Rental Property Investing

Residential Real Estate Investing for
Passive Income and Financial Freedom:
Finding and Financing Winning Deals,
Stress-Free Property Management, and
Building Wealth and Success

By Alexander S.

1st Edition. December 2023.

ISBN: 9798872124030

ACKNOWLEDGMENTS

I'm back with the second part of this investment book series. Thank you for the good reception of the first and for and for providing the motivation I needed to write this second part. In these guides I want to show you how my family and I have achieved financial freedom and how you can do it too.

It's been over 20 years since I became interested in investing. My gratitude to all the people who at some point asked for help, because thanks to you it has been possible to gather the knowledge that is in this book and that I can now and want to share with everyone who may find it useful.

The process of writing this book has been an exciting journey, and I hope it proves to be the same for you. Dedicated to my family and all the people who have encouraged me to write this second part.

TABLE OF CONTENTS

Acknowledgments 3

Introduction 7

Chapter 1 - Living off passive income: Deciphering the strategies and challenges of real estate investment 10

Chapter 2 - Investing for a better life: Balancing profitability and well-being 21

Chapter 3 - Start your path: Key concepts, investment categories and barrier management 26

Chapter 4 - Uncovering the secret of high profitability: Target prices, strategies and associated risks. 43

Chapter 5 - Financial strategies to boost your investments: Discover the keys to obtaining the best financing and scaling your business 72

Chapter 6 - Mastering the psychology of buyers and sellers: Effective strategies for negotiating home prices 86

Chapter 7 - The ideal tenant: Methods for ensuring success 100

Final Reflection 115

INTRODUCTION

I'm back with the second part of this series of investment guides where I want to show you how my family and I managed to achieve our financial freedom and how you are going to achieve it too. If you have not yet read the first part "Financial Freedom: Investing Guide to Getting Rich Step by Step with Index Funds, ETFs and Real Estate" I encourage you to do so, because all the secrets that I show you here are complementary with other investment methods.

Welcome to a fascinating journey into the world of investments, where the key is not only to accumulate savings but to invest intelligently and for the long term. With this book I intend to guide you towards building the plan that will lead you to financial independence, freeing you from the exclusive dependence on your job to cover your expenses. On this path, there are no shortcuts, only the certainty of slow but sure progress.

I will take you to the heart of financial management, sharing the lessons I've learned throughout my life from my mistakes, and extending an invitation for you to put this knowledge into practice alongside me.

This book is designed for all those who wish to practically understand the world of investments, and specifically the real estate investment method that is available to everyone. There is no age limit to discover these teachings; Each person can draw their own lessons from this book.

I already told you that we are a common family, and that we have given the importance it deserves to our personal finances. We have invested our savings year after year and in this way, we have achieved our financial freedom and we are meeting all our goals. Each person will have to define their own goals, which will serve as a motivator to not give up in moments of weakness.

Financial freedom is not achieved in four days, it is impossible. Since buying my first shares at the age of 24 and making my initial real estate investment at 28, I have explored various methods and have discovered the only viable approach: reading, studying, and applying knowledge. I've learned from my mistakes with dedication, effort, and perseverance.

This book is an invitation to an exciting journey, full of learning and opportunities where I will teach you how to invest in real estate safely and for the long term.

There are four of us at home. Our daughters are currently studying at university, we continue working hard, because we like it, it contributes to us and it makes us grow personally and professionally. We have different types of assets: variable income, fixed income and real estate investment in residential homes. Approximately half of our assets are real estate investments and the other half are stock market assets.

One aspect we appreciate most about real estate investing is that it provides us with recurring income that we can reinvest, allowing us the capability to create new opportunities, primarily depending on our ability to identify and execute them.

Becoming an expert in real estate investing in four days is impossible. However, in four days, or less, you can read this book. Books change thoughts and based on our thoughts we act. My name is Alexander and knowledge, method and perseverance are the ingredients you need.

Let's start! …

CHAPTER 1 - LIVING OFF PASSIVE INCOME: DECIPHERING THE STRATEGIES AND CHALLENGES OF REAL ESTATE INVESTMENT

We start by addressing some of the questions that many ask before investing in real estate:

How many apartments should I have to live on rent? What type of homes should I invest in to speed up the process? How long do I need to recover my investment? What necessary or unnecessary risks am I taking?

Invest in real estate and you will live on passive income. A perfect headline.

Short, powerful and with a spectacular effect for the audience. Plus, it's achievable. It certainly is. But beneath the headline, which is the tip of the iceberg, lies a huge piece of ice. Look:

Between garages and homes, at the time I write these words we have fifteen properties. All properties are long term rented in our case.

It was 2003. I bought a home for $200,000 and in 2006, just before the crisis, I sold it for $300,000. $100,000 gross profit in three years. Not bad to start with. But it turned out that it was pure luck. Buy by chance in a rising market and sell by chance at a critical moment.

However, from 2009 to 2014, the opposite occurred for me because the method I described only works when the housing prices grow by 15% annually. And that is something that does not usually happen.

When we confuse output with input, we may have problems. The output is the result. And it can be good because of good input (good prior work) or because of chance. And, be careful, because it can also be bad despite good input.

So now, drawing from almost twenty years of experience as a real estate investor, I will share my perspective on living off income from rented properties.

How many apartments should I have to live on rent? Calculations to live on income with real estate investment.

At the outset, we are going to define how much money you need to live on income. It is obvious that it depends on each particular case. Imagine an average annual salary of $36,000 net. So, let's set the goal of earning $3,000 a month. I'm not saying it's what you need. It is just an example to do the calculation.

The next question would be: To earn a net $3,000 per month, how many apartments do you need to rent? Forget about the rental income amounts. What truly matters here is what you have left in your pocket each month.

If you earn $6,000 per month in rent, but your expenses associated with those rents are $6,500 per month, you can imagine that with each passing day you need more money to maintain your investments.

Here we seek the opposite. We seek to generate $3,000 per month, which is the difference between monthly income and all monthly costs (including taxes).

Therefore, we are going to try to understand how many floors we need. There is a reality in real estate investment: the cheaper the home we buy, the more profitable (percentage-wise) it tends to be.

What rental price is always in high demand?

Let's think about a couple in which both of them earn a net monthly salary between them of $6,000. This implies that in their case they could allocate about $1,800 per month (30%) to rent, without many problems.

As they are a couple that thinks a lot about their future, they prefer to look for a home for around $1,400 a month. In this way they will be able to further increase their savings and investment. After all, they want to live only a few years of rent. Then they want to buy their own home. And who knows? Maybe even increase your family. So, let's think about rents of $1,400 a month.

Let's move on to the next question:

How much do homes that rent for $1,400 a month cost?

This is a critical question. The reality is that the price dispersion is very great. And this is the beauty of the real estate business. It is very easy to buy apartments that cost $340,000 or more that you can barely rent for $1,400 a month. In the same way, you can also find homes (although you will have to work much harder) in which you invest just $175,000 plus the corresponding taxes and also rent for $1,400 per month.

The second ones are older. They require more maintenance. They are in worse areas. They do not usually have an elevator and sometimes require some type of more or less important renovation. In large capitals it is very difficult to find homes for "only $175,000." But as you move away from them or look in less glamorous provincial capitals, it is easier to find this type of opportunity when you search with method and persistence.

The problem with these very profitable homes is that they are riskier. Risk of future spills and, above all, a greater risk for the tenant (although you can greatly reduce it if you use the method that I will tell you about in the final chapters of the book). The quality of the tenant is not that good. And that's why we know that the probability of default can increase.

We want to live off income, of course. But we also want to sleep with a certain peace of mind at night. Because going through life without having slept well is not a good plan either.

Let's assume that we are investors who seek profitability at the same time as having a good quality of night's sleep. For this reason, we are considering investments in homes of $250,000 (neither as cheap as those of $175,000 nor as expensive as those of $340,000) that we can rent for $1,400 per month (as an example, in one of my last pre-covid investments, I acquired a house priced at $285,000 and was quickly rented for $1,550 per month).

These are profitable investments that can carry a moderate to low risk if we make wise tenant selections. It is a possible scenario within a 30-mile radius of virtually every place in your country or region. So potentially it's something you could do.

The numbers speak for themselves.

You will examine them later in a table; for now, believe me and continue reading. One way to generate a monthly salary of $3,000 is to invest in ten homes with a cost of $275,000 each. Consider this!

And you're left thinking: "Ten homes to earn ONLY a salary of $3,000!" Don't go, now the party of details begins. And the details are always where the difference between a good investor and an average one exists.

I attach a table where I have summarized the main calculations of our typical investment:

Concept	Investment $250,000
Purchase price	$256,000
Monthly rent	$1,400
Monthly cash flow (approx.)	$280
Monthly equity increases due to debt amortization (approx.)	$510
Number of Homes for salary of $3,000	10 – 11 Homes (3,000/280)
Savings contributed for housing	$84,000

Total capital needed to obtain the monthly salary	$840,000
Initial debt for housing	$205,000
Total initial debt (if we bought all the homes at once)	$2,050,000

"Table. Main calculations of "our" typical investment."

As I have anticipated, a profitable investment (a $250,000 home rented for $1,400) and well managed puts almost $280 a month in our pocket (more than $3,300 annually).

But it is also evident that, if you look at the previous table, each year our assets additionally increase by another $6,240, which is the amount by which we reduce the debt.

So, if we do things right for the next thirty years, this house will generate this annual cash flow (assuming that neither the interest rate nor the rental income changes, which is already a lot to assume) and the house will be paid for.

At that moment "we will be in another dimension" and the monthly cash flows will be multiplied by three or even four since we will not have any associated mortgage.

But of course, it is thirty years (or the duration of the mortgage you have chosen, usually 20, 25 or 30 years, taking into account that, the shorter the duration of the mortgage, the lower the cash flow, but the greater the annual increase in assets due to amortization of mortgage debt).

15

What if I want to accelerate the process? We all desire speed, but sometimes, going too fast can lead to accidents. Let's explore how to speed up a bit.

The magic table: How to live off income by investing in rental apartments in a more accelerated way?

Therefore, if we want to 'earn' a monthly salary of $3,000, we need to invest in ten homes similar to the ones priced at $250,000 that I mentioned earlier.

Now we will see some ways to accelerate reaching that salary by investing in homes. But don't be fooled, some ways require much more time on your part than simple semi-passive management and some of them increase the risk considerably with the subsequent associated headaches.

Below, I show you a complete table so that you understand everything a little better. Let's analyze well the following table where you will see the numbers and returns depending on whether we invest in a home that costs us $175,000, $250,000 or $340,000:

Type of investment	Aggressive	Standard	Without negotiating or search
Purchase price	$175,000	$256,000	$340,000
Monthly rent	$1,400	$1,400	$1,400
Monthly cash flow (approx.)	$460	$280	$90
Monthly equity increases due to debt amortization (approx.)	$315	$510	*$620*
Number of Homes for salary of $3,000	6	11	33
Savings contributed for housing	$59,000	$84,000	$108,000
Total capital needed to obtain the monthly salary	$354,000	$924,000	$3,564,000
Initial debt for housing	$140,000	$205,000	$270,000

Total initial debt (if we bought all the homes at once)	$840,000	$2,255,000	$8,910,000
Asset risk	High	Half	Low
Debt risk	Low	Half	High
Housing liquidity	Low	Half	high
Management	Semi-passive	Passive	Passive
Strategy	Cash flow + equity	Cash flow + equity	Equity

"Table. How to live off income by investing in rental property?"

This table gives a lot to talk about. It is the table that I hope will clarify the path to your financial freedom by investing in rental apartments. How many apartments should I invest in if I want to generate a salary for myself? You see it. The table speaks for itself. Whether it's five, ten, or thirty properties, the difference lies in the type of homes you choose to invest in.

The cheaper the homes are, the faster you can generate those happy $3,000 per month for yourself. But look, like almost everything in life it is a double-edged sword. The cheapest apartments are the most profitable, but in part they are because they have a greater risk associated with them (by area, by type of home, by state of conservation...). Many sighs when they see these numbers and think: «If to have a salary like the majority, I need to invest in five, ten or thirty homes, this is very difficult, right? And in part, it is. They are right, investing in homes is not for everyone.

Make no mistake, it is not an issue for rich people. Nor is it only for young people under thirty who have their entire lives ahead of them. Not at all. I really don't think it's that. There are people 50-60 years old who have sold their primary home of 600,000 or 700,000 dollars that they had paid month after month for 30 years and have bought several homes and achieved financial freedom in one or two years (after a life of work and effort).

Investing in rental homes is made for those who are able to raise their heads and look at the long term. Those who are disciplined and who do not look for the quick shot.

The true magic of investing in rental homes.

See what happens if you raise your head a little. Every month you generate more than $300 of assets in the three types of investments that I have shown you. In the investments of the most economical apartments, the equity is mainly generated by cash flow. While in the most expensive ones you generate it especially due to the decrease in debt that automatically occurs month after month when you pay the mortgages associated with the investments.

In the two most favorable investment cases (the one with the floors of $175,000 and $250,000), if you add the benefits you obtain from the cash flows and the debt amortization at some point between the sixth and the tenth year you will have already recovered more than all your initial investment. And obviously you will continue to have an asset that generates cash flow and equity every month, both due to its appreciation in value and the decrease in its associated debt. Furthermore, you will see that a very important part (unlike other types of investment) of the result depends on you.

In real estate investing, almost everything depends on you, you are the CEO of your investments. In real estate investing you are the CEO of each investment. The risk is your ability to select, prepare and rent homes. This is why I like real estate investing so much.

If you do things well, your results depend little on the market and external factors and a lot on your management. In a few years the snowball can get bigger and bigger because your skill and knowledge will also grow.

CHAPTER 2 - INVESTING FOR A BETTER LIFE: BALANCING PROFITABILITY AND WELL-BEING

In recent years we have been acquiring an average of one home per year and in this way constantly increasing our real estate assets. We have done it at a moderate speed, in line with the rest of our activities, without haste. Learning and enjoying the path at the same time and acting in many moments in a stoic way to overcome the different difficulties that always arise when one climbs in the real estate business.

I'm not just going to highlight the nice and easy part of real estate investing because not everything is wonderful. Obviously, there is always an associated risk that we have to take into account. In my case, I am already over forty and I am fortunate to be very well accompanied by my family. I consider myself a cautious person and at a certain point I am not willing to take risks that endanger our family finances. I've been trying to play it safe for years.

It's not all numbers. Balance between profitability and well-being.

In the world of investment, it seems that everything is numbers. The numbers come out everywhere. And sometimes, too many numbers don't help us; they confuse us and do not let us see the holistic impact (economic, emotional, family...) of our investments. An example:

Something that is not objectively measurable when you invest is the suffering or mental stress that that certain investment causes you. It is not measurable simply because it depends on each investor. Each investor reacts differently to the problems and volatility that every investment has to overcome in order to bear certain fruits. No matter how passive your investment is, our mind is a specialist in creating stories about how it is evolving. If inflation appears to be starting to rise, we will think that our bonds will fall in value because central banks will raise interest rates. If a tenant in one of our home's delays paying us a couple of days, you can sleep poorly.

Each investment can bring suffering to us as investors if we do not know how to deal with it. For this reason, it is very useful not to take excessive risks and to focus on the long term to put into perspective all the decisions that real estate investors must make on a regular basis: renovations, tenants, financing...

For all these reasons, this is not a book that seeks the last dollar of profitability. No. This is a book that seeks a good balance between profitability and well-being. That seeks the sustainability of your real estate investments also from an emotional point of view.

If you want to live to be able to invest better, perhaps this is not the right book for you. If you want to invest to live better, probably yes. Let's start!

You have already seen in the table in the previous chapter that if you want to live on income with (relatively) little capital to contribute and a few apartments (six we have seen in the example) you should look for investments of around 175,000 dollars that rent for 1,400 dollars a month. Is this the right strategy for everyone? Probably not.

In general, greater risk, greater profitability and, on the contrary.

As with other types of investments, as we explain in my other book 'Financial Freedom,' investments are governed by the triangle of profitability, liquidity, and security. To get two of these three properties you have to lose the remaining one.

Passive/active management: Do you want to manage your apartments more passively or more actively?

Probably if you are willing to manage more actively you will be able to obtain greater profitability. Very small homes with a lot of tenant turnover, room rentals or vacation rentals are examples of more active real estate management that generate greater profitability than renting a home to a retired couple in which they will probably live until the end of their days.

Is risk always relative? Reduce the different uncertainties that exist and you will reduce the risks of each operation.

If you know an area very well, the area risk goes down. If you are a handyman, the risk of renovation goes down. If you work in a bank, the financing risk goes down. So, let's not go with ready-made formulas to calculate risk. The risk is mainly linked to the uncertainty that each new real estate opportunity generates for you.

The more uncertainty, the more risk you will take. Therefore, the job of a good real estate investor is to reduce uncertainty in decision-making. I leave you some examples:

1. If you invest in a block that you don't know, there is uncertainty about knowing what the neighbors and the community will be like. What should you do to reduce that uncertainty?

   Answer: ask everyone: neighbors, community, real estate agency, nearby bars and even the cats that walk around at night. This way you reduce uncertainty.

2. How much will a potential operation rent for? Again, there is uncertainty.

   Answer: question, question and question. Sometimes you will be able to reduce uncertainty a lot and sometimes only a little. Throughout my life I have met other investors who have even published false ads (before buying the home) to estimate demand (in my case, it does not seem the most appropriate).

3. And to reduce the uncertainty of a certain reform?

   Answer: ask several workers and companies and ask for quotes. In any case, until you do your first renovations you will not be a crack at estimating renovation costs.

   But make no mistake. If you buy with a good margin of safety, you have room to make small estimation errors.

4. Liquidity: What if you need to transform your homes into money?

   Answer: There are many types of housing. Some much more liquid than others. And above all, you must be aware that there are homes in which once you invest, it is very difficult to get out of that investment quickly and transform it back into money.

   This usually happens, especially with homes with significant deficits. Be very aware of this point. For example: By investing in a home without an elevator and that is more than fifty years old, you will pay much less than in a similar home with an elevator and parquet on the floor. But, if for whatever reason you need to sell your investment, it may take much longer to find a buyer compared to other homes. Or not. You never know. Each case is a story.

In short, the better the home, the greater the liquidity.

Ten years ahead: a strategy that rarely fails.

Investing in profitable homes (those of 175,000 or 250,000 dollars that generate 1,400 dollars per month in rent) to rent for more than ten years almost never fails. And do you know why? Ten years from now you will normally be able to live through more than one economic cycle. And in almost every full period you will have additional gains from home value appreciation.

In any case, in the examples we have given. In that period, you have already paid all your initial investment. And therefore, you have an asset that generates cash and equity every month regardless of the fluctuation in its market value.

Furthermore, ten years from now, you can gradually acquire more homes. Slowly but surely. As your experience increases, you learn to reduce the risk of each operation and therefore you can scale with much more security.

And remember, at thirty years (or twenty or twenty-five years, depending on the length of your mortgage) the $3,000 per month becomes more than $9,000 per month and that is without taking into account the increase in prices due to inflation. The magic is that the mortgage is gone and all its associated costs (like life insurance) are gone too. From 3,000 to 9,000 dollars per month. That would change the lives of many.

Furthermore, the end of mortgages usually coincides with periods of less professional activity and therefore is a complement to a potential public pension.

Yes, you like to walk and take life at your own pace, welcome to the exciting world of real estate investment.

CHAPTER 3 - START YOUR PATH: KEY CONCEPTS, INVESTMENT CATEGORIES AND BARRIER MANAGEMENT

In the previous chapter we have seen the general idea of how to live off income. The basic numbers and especially the number of homes needed depending on the type of profitability we are looking for in each home to be able to achieve a certain monthly income.

Now, we will not focus on the key elements. What type of floor is right for you? To what extent is it healthy to get into debt? With what mentality to face the fears that arise naturally when buying for the first time?

Below, I show you the most important thing you should know before buying your first home as an investment. The first time is always the most challenging, particularly from an emotional standpoint. For this reason, I have delved into the three most important factors that you should take into account before making your first investment:

1. The four ways in which you will increase your assets through the purchase of an apartment.
2. The three types of apartments to acquire based on a mental model that I have created and that follows from the previous chapter, with all its advantages and disadvantages to find the one that best suits your personal situation or your objectives.
3. The fears that will naturally arise in you and how to overcome

them.

What profitability can I obtain when investing in an apartment to rent?

The answer is typically 3-10% (without taking into account the additional returns you get from leverage). But you should know that the profitability you obtain will basically depend on the type of home you invest in. And therefore, establishing a mental model with a classification of apartments based on their profitability can be helpful.

The four ways in which you will increase your assets by investing in apartments to rent.

Before buying your first home as an investment and renting it out, you must understand well the four formulas with which a real estate investment increases your assets:

1. **Home appreciation.** Do your parents have a home worth ten times what it cost them forty years ago? How many times have we heard this phrase? This effect is called inflation.

   Inflation is the cheapest way for a state to reduce the value of its debt. States are in debt and therefore they are the most interested in the value of their debt falling. This fact causes inflation in the economy, which increases the monetary value of assets.

   Many speculators invested with the sole expectation that property values would rapidly increase, driven by short-term profits, which was a common strategy from 2003 to 2007. The end result was the ruin of many of them.

   The appreciation of the property should be an extra prize to the investment you make in real estate. It should not be the main reason that supports your investment.

2. **Cash flow.** Cash flow is the difference between the money

that goes out to pay for your investment and the money that comes in. When the difference is positive, your investment has positive cash flow and therefore makes your pockets bigger as time goes by.

If you find yourself consistently putting money out of your pocket each month or year to sustain the investment, it results in negative cash flow.

How many investments can you make with positive cash flow? Infinite

How many investments can you make with negative cash flow? The ones that your pocket can hold.

There is no need to add much more. Look for real estate investments with positive cash flows if you want to invest in real estate profitably for a long time.

3. **Tax advantages.** The governments of almost all countries in the world are interested in ensuring that the supply of primary residences for rent does not decline, as this would cause a social problem (even greater than the current one) that is difficult to manage.

Therefore, it is possible that in your country or region there are tax incentives for investors who promote long-term primary residence rentals.

4. **Amortization of the home.** The tenants of the house pay us rent. That rent, if we have made a good investment, generates a positive cash flow. But in addition to that, when paying the mortgage payment every month, the rent itself pays us the interest and the corresponding part of the capital.

The part of capital that we pay with the rent that the tenant pays us monthly is the fourth factor. With each passing month we owe the bank less money. If you think about it coldly, when you make a good real estate investment, you buy a home only with the initial money (down payment). You pay the entrance fee and everything else will be paid for by the tenants. Moreover, if you succeed in making an investment with positive cash flow, your tenants will not only cover all expenses but also contribute additional funds to your pocket.

Remember a couple of details:

- The one who mortgages for twenty or thirty years is the investor. And that debt, no matter what happens, must be paid. By the way, if the investor dies, he remains "inheritable."
- If you are not able to rent the apartment, you must continue paying the mortgage. So, you can now begin to understand that for the magic to happen, the choice of home is critical. And to choose a good home, I present to my friends the mental models. You'll see how they will help us make a good choice.

The importance of mental models and what they are for.

When looking for an apartment to invest in, it helps to have a simple model in mind that classifies your potential investments. Therefore, I have created a mental model with three types of apartments in which to invest. In my case, understanding that there are three investment types helps me be much more efficient in the search and negotiation.

As I have briefly mentioned previously, depending on your investment strategy, it is reasonable to expect gross returns ranging from 3% to 10%. And all this without counting leverage. Once we leverage ourselves, obviously the returns can skyrocket (up and exceed double digits if the operation goes well and also down if the operation does not go as we had thought).

That is why, in view of simplification, I have divided the investment options that we can undertake into three types of housing based on their

29

potential profitability.

The three categories of the mental model that will help you better select your real estate investments.

1. Conservative investment.

An apartment where everyone would like to live. Neutral or slightly negative cash flow. 3-4% gross profitability.

Investing in apartments with returns of 3 or 4 percent is quite common. Many real estate investors are comfortable with this type of investment because it generally involves little risk. Basically, investors replicate the model they have used to purchase their primary home. They perform practically the same steps. They search in the same area and look for characteristics similar to what they have or what they would like.

It usually leads to very few errors because when we buy a first home, we know the area and the prices very well. In our neighborhood we know exactly the difference between a good or very good area, the communities with the most problems or even the bars that make the most noise. Therefore, they are investments that actually do not have much risk, although the profitability is low.

In any case, the important thing is to know that in these homes the cash flow is usually neutral in the best of cases. And that does NOT allow the model to be scaled. Since each new home of this type that you add to your assets increases the need to put money out of your pocket.

Let's take a real example of one of my homes:

- Cost of the home + 2 parking spaces: $750,000 (without taxes; mortgage of 80% real estate value).

- Monthly rent: $2,800.

- Monthly fixed rate mortgage at 2% for 30 years: $2,330

(currently $1,280 amortization + $1,050 interest).

- Monthly community: $230/month.

- IBI + Home and Life Insurance: $150/month.

- Monthly cashflow (when there are no unforeseen events): +$2,800 $ - $2,330 - $230 - $150 = +$90/month = what is eaten for what is served.

When there are unforeseen events, the cash flow becomes negative. Therefore, in this type of investment the gain is only capital (there is no generation of cash flows while the apartment is mortgaged). In the best of cases, the rent pays for the apartment.

The key is that you understand that each month that passes your amortized capital increases. Let's not be extremists. After all, it's not so bad. You pay an entry fee for a fantastic apartment. You mortgage yourself. And after thirty years (or however long you have the mortgage) you have an asset that the tenants have paid for you (except for the down payment and all incidentals) and with a much higher value than the one you bought (the power of inflation).

In general, you are buying an asset of high quality and little risk. This is the formula used by the majority of investors who purchase one or two apartments in addition to their usual home.

The problem with this type of real estate investment is that it does not scale well because we cannot have infinite apartments like this. Generating a neutral cash flow does not generate a sufficient safety margin. If we had a thousand apartments like these, we would end up ruined because there would be years in which unforeseen events would destroy our cash position.

If the cashflow of the initial investment is already negative, I do not recommend it at all, because then an investment with a low-moderate risk becomes a bad investment that takes away your cash for twenty or thirty years.

Be very careful with gross returns below 3.5%because they can generate negative cash flows for decades.

When making this type of investment, I recommend a fixed-rate mortgage because fixed rates generate investment certainty. You will always know what you pay. If you have a lot of savings that you could use to pay off the mortgage if interest rates rise in the future, you can extract an extra return using a variable interest mortgage.

If you use a fixed rate mortgage, the only variable in the equation that is out of your hands is what you deposit. And better to stop controlling one than two variables. This is my personal way of seeing it.

2. Moderate investment.

A flat that is good, but has some drawbacks. Positive cash flow. 5-6% gross profitability.

They are apartments that generally range from 185,000 to 350,000 dollars. They are in areas that the investor knows and their rents range from 1,200 to 1,750 dollars per month. In general, there is always some drawback that makes the profitability higher than that of the previous category.

Sometimes it's about their size. Too small for a family to consider living in them for a long time. Other times it has little light, the distribution is not ideal... Or it simply turns out that it is a very old apartment.

Let's give another real example of one of my homes within this category:

- Housing cost: $185,000 (without taxes; mortgage of 70% real estate value).

- Monthly rent: $1,620.

- Monthly fixed rate mortgage at 1.7% for 20 years: $950.

- Monthly community: $85/month.

- IBI + Home and Life Insurance: $115/month.

- Monthly cash-flow when the stars align and there are no unforeseen events: + $1,620 - $950 - $85 = + $585/month.

Of the three apartment categories that I show you in my mental model, they are, in my opinion, the most liquid apartments because they are buyable by investors and permanent tenants (although remember that, by definition, apartments have little liquidity). Its price-profitability formula is attractive because it greatly exceeds existing inflation.

These floors generate positive cash flow, even taking into account unforeseen events. Look in the real example how it generates $585 a month in cash flow. In this case we pay 30% plus taxes up front. That is, just over $116,000.

Conceptually, we could buy as many apartments as we wanted in this category or as many as our debt capacity would allow us, because each apartment that we add to our portfolio provides us with additional monthly income that the banks will take into account when requesting a new loan.

It is a strategy that carries moderate risk. In general, they are apartments that do not need to be renovated excessively (sometimes a small facelift is enough) and that are compatible with the work of most mortals since they do not need as much dedication as those in the next category.

3. Aggressive investment.

An apartment for less than $180,000. Very positive cashflow. 7-10% gross profitability or higher.

Putting the correct name to concepts helps process them. Let's imagine that a couple in the US can earn about 6,000 dollars a month. If you can or want to dedicate between 20 and 30% of your monthly disposable income to rent, it means that you have between $1,150 and $1,750 per month in rent to rent.

It is important to adapt this reasoning to the area where you plan to invest. It is always easier if it is close to your home (which does not mean it has to be precisely your city) because you have greater knowledge of the area.

This analysis starts from the demand and we observe that, for a couple, the average annual rental income is in the range of 14,000 to 18,000 dollars.

Therefore, if we want to obtain a gross annual return of more than 7%, we observe how the $230,000 of the total investment marks a reasonable upper limit.

Let's give another real example of one of my homes within this category:

- Housing cost: $137,000 (without taxes; mortgage of 75% real estate value).

- Monthly rent: $1,175.

- 2% fixed rate monthly mortgage for 25 years: $412.

- Monthly community: $70/month.

- IBI + Home and Life Insurance: $70/month.

- Monthly cash-flow (when there are no unforeseen events): + $1,175 - $412 - $70 - $70 = + $623/month.

We pay the entrance fee plus taxes. Just over $45,000. And the monthly flow is very good. Only the gross profitability by cash flow (relative to the down payment we pay) is more than 10%.

I know what you're thinking. But where I live, apartments that cost less than $230,000 are bad apartments.

Clear. That's the key, which is to turn a bad home into a habitable apartment. The trick is, perhaps, to reform and do a major facelift. Perhaps, in taking advantage of an asymmetry of power (you can afford not to buy an apartment and the person who sells due to lack of other offers cannot afford not to sell it to you).

We have to see many apartments for less than $230,000 and analyze them with the eyes of an investor (not with those eyes that we use when we think about showing a home to our relatives) and find that opportunity in which our ability as negotiators or our ability as reformers can create the magic necessary to transform a home that is sold in the low price range into a home for a family.

Perhaps depending on the area where you live, the $180,000 that names the category will become $230,000 or $140,000. You must adapt the threshold depending on your investment area. The important thing is that you understand the concept.

In which category of mental model homes do you want to invest? To what extent do you want to scale your number of homes?

First you must internalize and understand what type of housing you want to invest in. From here, start the search, discarding from the outset everything that you have not preselected.

Buying a nice apartment is very easy. Buying a profitable apartment requires an investor mentality that is important to acquire. To help you in your choice, I have made a simple table where I relate some important attributes of real estate investment with the typology of investment apartments that I have created in the mental model.

Type of investment	Cash flow	Appreciation long-term	Liquidity
Conservative	Negative or neutral	Does it equal inflation?	Very Low. Purchasable mainly by tenants.
Moderate	Positive	Does it equal inflation?	Low. Purchasable by investors and by tenants.
Aggressive	Very positive	Difficult to predict, but they age worse. What is the long-term impact of not having an elevator or basic elements? Be careful with the cost of the necessary reforms.	Very Low. Purchasable mainly by investors. In periods of crisis, it can be difficult to sell even at very low prices.

"Table. Advantages and disadvantages depending on the type of housing"

Each type of apartment in the mental model has advantages and disadvantages that you must take into account when choosing which type of apartment to invest in.

If you are not clear about what you want and if you do not fully understand the benefits and risks that each type of investment entails, you will end up being greatly influenced by the expertise of the apartment salesperson on duty.

Or, even worse, because of your senses, which will naturally lean towards the least profitable apartments since, as happens in life and as Michael Lewis demonstrated in his excellent book "Moneyball", what is aesthetically beautiful is overrated while what is aesthetically pleasing is overrated. It is more difficult for them to value what is undervalued (this same effect occurs in people and apartments).

Controlling your debt is critical to creating your real estate assets. Each person has an amount of mortgage credit that they can use (and I recommend that you use it responsibly). That credit is limited. It can be more or less depending on your age and your income mainly. But in any case, it has a limit.

If you use that credit to finance your main home, then you will have less left to invest in rental apartments. And if you use that credit to finance your real estate investments, then you will have less left to buy your main home.

It is very curious, but you should know that the size of your available credit also varies depending on whether you use the credit to invest or for your main home.

If you use the credit to invest it will be larger. Your leverage capacity will be greater. The reason is that banks allow you to extend credit whenever your income increases and, therefore, if you invest in properties that generate monthly income, the banks will verify that your income increases and, consequently, will give you more credit.

Anyway, keep an eye on it. There is a trick. Banks only check this after the fact. Never a priori. That is, if you have a rented home, you will now be able to prove your income to the bank (through the rental contract and the corresponding receipts). But if you don't have it rented yet (because it is your first purchase as an investment) the banks do not take into account those future inflows of money.

It is an important nuance. And now you ask me: "Why are you telling me all this?" Because there is only one life. Imagine that you exhaust all your mortgage credit with your real estate investments. And you do it very well. And you are one of the investors who buy apartments for less than $180,000 because you already know that the key is to buy cheap. And then you meet a person and decide to move in together.

And your partner wants to buy something together. Well, I'm sorry, but maybe it can't be. If your credit has run out and you don't have the money in the bank, you won't be able to buy the apartment of your dreams with your partner.

Obviously, there are solutions such as selling some of your investments. But keep in mind that profitable homes are usually less liquid than unprofitable ones, as I have already explained.

They are ironies of the market. Everyone wants a type of housing and for this reason, that type of housing becomes unprofitable, because demand drives up the price. So, understanding each person's personal situation and the concept of available credit is important.

Trying to expand your real estate credit (buying to invest first and then for your primary home) is a strategy that can work for younger people.

That's why being clear about each person's priorities is always so important.

Analyzing the jumps in profitability.

Miracles do not exist. Anyone who wants to buy on the main street of a capital, with a gross profitability of 10% because he is a very good negotiator or because he knows how to reform it, has two options:

1. Wait seated.
2. Let me know and we'll buy it halfway.

We have already classified the profitability of homes into 3 types.

A skilled investor can make a 'conservative investment' and achieve a 6% return. A very skillful investor can make a "moderate investment" and get a 7-8% gross return. And a crack investor can make an "aggressive investment" and get an 11% gross return.

Leaps in profitability can be achieved. But only from one category to the next. You can't skip two categories at once (in a legal way of course).

Transforming a "conservative investment" and getting a 9% return on it is practically impossible. It can happen, but they are very exceptional and are never the basis of a strategy to follow.

You can invest your entire life in looking for these opportunities and then you will end up tired and with a non-existent real estate portfolio.

Or you can start by investing in one of the categories you choose (ideally 2 or 3) and, as you progress and learn, try to be more sophisticated and jump a category in terms of profitability.

You choose. As usual. Action or paralysis by analysis.

Buy without putting capital?

I get in a very bad mood when I see advertisements from ruthless souls who preach from the rooftops that you can (and almost should) buy apartments without putting a euro out of your pocket.

The famous OPM (Other People Money) that obviously boosts your profitability if the play goes well. The return on invested capital (ROI) goes to infinity since it is a ratio between profit and money invested.

The problem is when the play doesn't go well. So obviously the profitability goes to at least infinity.

I'll be direct. A person who, for whatever reason, does not have savings at a given time should not get into the mess of buying an apartment to rent without a single euro. Please. A little common sense.

Can we buy an apartment without putting a euro out of our pocket? Well of course yes. And it can be very profitable if you know how to do it well. But do you know who can do that? He who has somewhat full pockets can do that.

So, investing without putting a single euro down is an option for those who have many dollars left over. Without further ado. It seems ironic, but it is not.

It is as simple as understanding that the riskiest investments must be part of a broad portfolio and where the weight of these investments in relation to the total is small.

Real estate investment includes moments where cash is needed. Moments that were not in the initial plan. There are unforeseen events that must be addressed, periods with the apartment empty or simply moments where the tenant does not pay you. Therefore, it is always necessary to have an emergency fund in the form of a box to be able to address those moments that usually come when one is less prepared than ever.

And if you buy the first apartment you buy without excess cash, the chances that the investment will not turn out well increase considerably. And it's a shame because you'll miss out on a great way to build wealth. Just because it started early and in the wrong way.

Buy gradually. Diversification in time and knowledge.

The problem with investing in apartments is that it greatly complicates diversification (both temporal and monetary). The amounts to invest are important and that is why I recommend starting with small investments. It is better to buy two homes for $163,000 to start than one for $320,000. The first option allows you to learn faster and make cheaper mistakes.

In my case, what gave me the necessary confidence was the very profitable purchase of a home for $140,000 and in the next home, together with my wife, we dared with an amount of more than $230,000.

Everything happened gradually, a few years passed and we consolidated learnings. We also increased our cash position with income from other sources.

Consistency is the most important thing. Speed is not relevant in an investment that takes decades or decades to mature.

How to manage the fears that always exist in the first real estate investments?

Our mind is designed to alert us and therefore to be able to survive. So, when you borrow tens or hundreds of thousands of dollars from the bank to create your real estate empire, a good head starts shooting with ideas that can boycott our investment or, worse yet, turn it into a source of constant nightmares.

Fears are normal and natural. What are the most common fears?

- "The interest rate is very low, what if it goes up?" Fixed interest mortgage. Final point.

- "What if it keeps going down and then I miss the cheap interest party?" Then you are sinning from ambition. Nobody is able to predict the market.

- "What if house prices go down in the next five years?" If you invest to speculate you have a problem. If you invest for the long term (more than ten years at least in real estate) then you have an opportunity to buy even more. Also, remember that historically the price of the cheapest rentals has fallen less than the price of homes. If you expect profitability throughout your life, you don't care too much if at certain times the price of housing drops.

- "What if they don't pay the rent?" Non-payment insurance.

- "What if they occupy my apartment?" It occurs very little in percentage terms, but apply the answer to the previous question, which also works. And if it happens, you should know that typical vacancy costs are usually around $7,000.

- "What if a meteorite falls that unexpectedly diverted its trajectory when passing near Pluto and a fragment fifty meters in diameter falls right on my home and destroys it? That!".

41

In the real estate rental game, you have to understand that the biggest risk that exists is that your apartment is not rentable. That is, you can't even rent it by lowering the price. Therefore, when you buy to invest, buy in an area where there is demand and where you think there may continue to be demand in the future (no one knows that, but there are areas with greater probabilities than others).

More profitable assets or other quality?

Apartments, like companies, also have different qualities. A flat without an elevator is usually more profitable (if you can rent it of course). It is more profitable because you pay less for the community (the elevator is one of the most expensive costs in a community) and also because the purchase price is much lower. In return, it is a less liquid asset and probably ages worse.

In our case we invest with the time horizon of never having to sell. Therefore, we mainly lean towards assets of type 2 of the mental model (moderate) with returns of 5-7%.

We like the fact that they are typically active less than twenty years old and think they can age well over the next thirty or forty years. In addition, maintenance time is less and we appreciate it because we like to dedicate our time to other activities.

But obviously we give up some profitability. We are conscious. And you? Are you clear about what you're playing? Do you want the Champions of profitability or do you prefer something less profitable and reduce the risk a little? Remember that if you want everything, you usually end up getting nothing.

I hope this chapter is useful to take a step forward. Congratulations for making it this far! We continue!

CHAPTER 4 - UNCOVERING THE SECRET OF HIGH PROFITABILITY: TARGET PRICES, STRATEGIES AND ASSOCIATED RISKS.

In the preceding two chapters, we discussed the significance of identifying investments with substantial profitability and positive cash flow.

Numerous methods exist for discovering rental apartments with high profitability. However, it is crucial not to overlook the associated risks, which need careful analysis and, above all, effective management. We are going to see ten different strategies to achieve high profitability in renting homes.

One of the most frequently asked questions from novice investors is how to locate the real estate opportunities that many discuss (but few discover) that consistently yield double-digit returns.

The first thing I want to announce to you is that every time I read a headline online explaining how to achieve double-digit performance, I become suspicious. And you should too.

In most cases they are articles of poor content, inaccurate and based on exceptional conditions of the past. In this case it will be different, we will see relevant and easy to understand content.

The content in this chapter can be categorized into three main sections:

- First steps to take and ten strategies you can use to achieve those returns.

- We will analyze the risks associated with these high returns.

- And to illustrate and work with numbers at the end of the book I will show you a real example.

Get comfortable, and let's begin the search.

Determine the minimum rental price in your investment area.

The first step, as almost always, is to investigate. We must find the minimum rental price in the area where you want to invest (ideally less than 30 kilometers from your usual home, especially if you are starting out to facilitate rental management).

When you analyze any type of investment you must understand where the profitability comes from. And if there is a very important extra profitability compared to the average profitability of the asset, you must understand even more the main causes of that extra profitability. There is always some reason that can explain extra profitability.

In the case of investing in rental properties, a phenomenon occurs that is reproduced in all areas. There is a minimum rental price below which rental opportunities are scarce:

- In the big capitals perhaps that price is $1,400 a month (in the humblest neighborhoods).

- In other metropolitan areas perhaps that price is lower and stands at $1,050 per month.

- And there are also towns and cities with less demand since there are fewer job opportunities where the minimum rent for a home is between 800-950 dollars per month.

It is crucial that, in the area (including the neighborhood, obviously) where you want to invest (remembering that the real estate market is highly localized), you comprehend that minimum rental price. It is very easy to get it. You just have to do a search on the real estate portals and sort by rental price. Disregard the destroyed homes for rent (I put my hands on my face when I see those ads) and you will quickly see that many rentals are concentrated at a very similar low price.

Voila! You already have it. You have now found the usual minimum rental price for the area where you want to invest. There is a minimum price at which any apartment that is in good condition for living could be rented.

Determining the maximum purchase price, you should pay for a home.

Once you know that minimum price, you could extract the maximum purchase price by looking for a certain profitability. For example:

- The minimum rental price in your area is $1,200 per month, so you know you can get a double-digit return if your investment doesn't exceed $144,000. It is calculated: ($1,200 x 12 months / 144,000) x 100 = 10%. Difficult to find, but as we will see later, it is not impossible to find.

- On the other hand, if the minimum rental price in your area is $800 per month, you know that you will be able to obtain a high double-digit return if your investment does not exceed $96,000. It could also be calculated like this: $800 x 12 months x 10 (if you want 10%, if you want 12% for example, you only have to change this last number to obtain the maximum purchase price).

The main challenge is that, upon analyzing the actual cost of apartments compared to rental income, it becomes evident that opportunities are scarce in high-profitability areas. In fact, in many cases they have to be created.

There are apartments that cost twice as much as others (or even more) that can be rented for practically the same price. It is important to understand this reality. In general, the prices of portal advertisements do not allow us to find these high returns. High profitability opportunities are not abundant and therefore we will have to use some strategies that we will see later to be able to access them.

In summary, we've learned that understanding the minimum rental price helps you define your purchase budget limit. Now let's go to the next question:

How can I find apartments as affordable as the ones you're suggesting?

Now that you have understood that the key to the process is not to exceed a certain purchase price and to obtain a purchase price that is below the market price, let's see what strategies you can use to achieve this.

Before you begin your search, it's important to realize that the best opportunities often lie outside your comfort zone. I'm sorry to tell you that finding good real estate opportunities is possible, but it requires some effort. Like almost everything worthwhile in life.

But the most important effort is the mental one because to find good returns you will have to eliminate prejudices by investing, perhaps, in areas that you did not expect, receive many no's to offers that for the other party will not make sense, visit apartments that were built before your parents. were born or manage a group of workers who help you renovate an apartment to add value.

Homes that are "move-in ready" tend to be less profitable. People seek comfort and avoid the possible inconveniences of a renovation.

Now, we start the search. Change your mindset, keep an open mind and remember that the magic of high profitability is somewhere you haven't visited in a while. Will you accompany me?

Ten different ways to find highly profitable homes.

1.- Floors in zones C on a scale of ABCD zones.

Don't look for homes in the most commercial streets of your city. Don't even think about looking on the street where all the criminals hang out. Changing the "goodness" or "badness" of a neighborhood will be impossible for you! And even if the neighborhood changes, if that neighborhood has a "reputation as a difficult neighborhood, that reputation will take generations to disappear." Therefore, avoid the worst zones (the D zones on an ABCD scale).

On the other hand, in humble and working-class areas (type C areas) is where you will find the greatest opportunities with the least risk. Lifelong neighborhoods. The kind where when the children leave home, they look for a small apartment in the same neighborhood so they can be close to their loved ones. These are neighborhoods that have been in demand for sixty or seventy years. It would be rare for demand to diminish in the coming decades.

The recommendation is that you be very rational in this regard. Many real estate investors live in zones A or zones B and precisely for this reason it is difficult for them to invest in zones C. If you are looking for high profitability sometimes it is best to get out of your comfort zone, swallow all your prejudices and be as rational as possible in the search for the most profitable neighborhood with the least possible risk (type C neighborhoods).

Therefore, my recommendation is that you carefully analyze the map of neighborhoods of the city where you want to invest. Try to classify each neighborhood in a classification from A to D and focus on zones C. Each neighborhood is very different so if you invest outside your neighborhood (because you live in zone A or B) try to know the different subzones that make up that neighborhood you have selected.

As for areas A. Being able to tell your friends that you live in the best neighborhoods in your city comes at a price. You are signaling to the world "that things are going well for you." Like someone who buys a

Rolex to know what time it is. And that price is paid much more by the owner than by the tenant. For this reason, the returns of the best areas are worse.

Everyone wants a flat there and prices skyrocket. The risk is obviously lower. On Saturday night you will look like a champion when you have beer and a glass of "Albariño", but at the end of the month, when you collect the rent, you will barely have enough to pay the mortgage and little more if you have bought at the majority price.

In terms of rental housing profitability, working-class neighborhoods tend to be winning bets.

2.- Old floors.

One of our investments. In an old renovated apartment with a simple but effective "facelift". Older apartments are cheaper. And it's normal. Because they have less useful life. Remember that floors "wear out." Like erasers. Yes, yes! Like rubber bands. There is also a moment when there is nothing left (well, just the terrain).

And at that moment maybe you have to build everything again. If the floor is of good quality, perhaps the construction will last one hundred and fifty years. If the construction is fairer, it will cost it to reach the centenary age.

So, when you purchase an old apartment, you acquire less useful life and incur higher maintenance costs. But you know what? It usually pays off.

It compensates because new apartments have a price premium much higher than those costs that I mention. And it's normal. Because humans are very emotional and we decide through our senses and intuition.

And the best? If you buy an old apartment and give it a facelift and it looks new (or semi-new inside) you have the advantages of paying the price of an old apartment and being able to charge (almost) the rent for a new apartment.

Maybe the renovation or facelift is not worth it. Or maybe yes. You will have to do numbers. But, to begin with, I recommend something that I see that some do not comply with. When you place an ad on real estate portals, paint the entire apartment before taking the photos you post.

The advantage is that you only need to paint it once, preferably in light colors or white; it's easy on the eyes and generally well-received. If you paint it the first time, the other times the tenants will paint it for you because (if you specify it clearly in the rental contract) they will leave the apartment the same as they found it (and if they don't leave it painted for you, you will appropriate their deposit money legally as stated in the contract).

So, paint the apartment the first time please, take some good photos and your old apartment will look much better and you will rent it for much more.

3.- Homes without elevator.

All the homes my wife and I own, except for one, have an elevator. It's amusing because both she and I try to avoid elevators whenever possible. But of course, when our daughters were little, we left the house as if we were on vacation for two weeks and obviously when we were loaded, we used the elevator.

In any case, we have the typical problem of behavioral bias and perhaps we do not understand that there are many situations in which an elevator barely adds value. Imagine that you are twenty-five years old, have a fair salary, and someone asks you the following question:

Would you rather have an elevator and pay 120 dollars a month more in rent or not have it and be able to use those 120 dollars? The answer is that many will probably answer that they prefer $120 a month.

It is important that we not be blinded by the bias of our behavior. Apartments without elevator are usually much more profitable because:

- <u>Its acquisition price is much cheaper</u> (In many cases they can cost half the price, and the rent you charge is much more than half if you have an elevator).

- <u>The community cost is much lower.</u> Depending on how many neighbors you have, you can save $50 a month or even more. And all that savings goes into your pocket in the form of a benefit since remember that the community cost is paid by the owner.

Now, you must take into account two important factors (what you should put in the risk part of the risk-return balance):

- <u>Homes without an elevator are less liquid.</u> If you want to sell an apartment without an elevator, it will cost you many more months (on average) than if it does not have one (it is not only a matter of lowering the price, since the market for apartment seekers without an elevator is much smaller and is mainly composed of investors).

- The time it will take to rent the apartment may also be longer if the area in which you have the apartment is not in high demand. You can simulate this in your numbers with an increase in the time of the empty floor.

In summary, the elevator is a great invention that usually subtracts some profitability points, although it provides more liquidity to the investment, as it facilitates the sale of the property if necessary.

4.- Find an inherited apartment with different heirs.

In many instances, heirs want to sell the apartment quickly, and the calculations are swift. If ten brothers inherit an apartment worth $100,000, when they sell it, each brother will get $10,000 less the corresponding taxes. If the apartment is not sold for a while, arguments could arise: those who have money will pretend that the issue does not concern them nor does it matter to them. Total, for 10,000 dollars and those who need it urgently need the sale.

So, when an inheritance takes a while to sell is when there are great opportunities for discounts. Because lowering the price of a $100,000 apartment by inheritance by 40% is not lowering the price by $40,000, it is lowering "only" $4,000 per sibling (if there are 10 siblings, for example).

If you find inheritances out there. Do the heirs a favor. Make a downward offer. Keep the apartment and solve the family problem. It's a win/win without a doubt.

5.- Bank housing.

Banks make money by lending and charging interest above the cost, not by holding properties on their balance sheets. So, the banks have a problem (one more). And fat. Because in their balance sheets they also record (for example) that an apartment has a value of (for example) 200,000 dollars when in reality it is worth 140,000 dollars (which is what the client is willing to pay). But since the banks are listed on the stock market, they do not lower the price of apartments suddenly. Every year they provision (lowering the price of their balance sheet) little by little.

This way they save time and can generate profits every year (although each year that passes, the year they are weaker; you just have to look at the banks' quotes, they seem like a joke).

Bank floors are, perhaps, the floors in which it is easiest to negotiate as long as there is no excess demand for a certain floor. Because on his part there is no emotion. There is no type of bond or attachment. In the bank there is a system with an asset valued at a price. Final point. The bank salesperson or analyst has not lived his childhood there.

The bank's salesperson (who is normally part of a marketing company) wants to sell you the apartment. And he wants to sell it at the price the central office analyst allows.

So, shoot out offers and, if you persevere, you might be able to get a good price. At the end of the year perhaps even better because they have annual objectives to meet and they need to reach sales, even if it is at a lower price. The annual accounts are too important to want to extract the last euro from a non-productive asset.

6.- Avoid very touristy areas. Prioritize metropolitan areas

Investing in tourist apartments can be highly profitable, but it's a different business. It is a much more intensive business in management hours. Hours that you can outsource to companies that will charge you a service fee, which will obviously mean that your potential profitability will be lower. Or hours that you will dedicate yourself if you have a lot of free time (unscalable business if you do it this way).

Furthermore, when renting apartments for tourism, depending on your country or region, it is possible that you do not have tax deductions (find out what the situation is in your case).

The objective of this book is not to compare profitability between tourist rentals or long-term rentals. So, I won't go into detail. But you should know that they are different businesses and, above all, three of them have very different potential returns.

The problem is that if you buy apartments for long-term rental in very touristy areas you are playing the worst real estate game possible. Because you invest in an extremely expensive place and on top of that you will not benefit from the potential high income from tourist rentals.

It is one thing for you to buy a second home, enjoy it during your vacation periods and dedicate the rest of the time to renting it. And another is that you invest in a habitual residence in a tourist area. The numbers won't work for you. Avoid those areas if you are looking for a good return.

7.- Convert two-bedroom apartments into three-bedroom apartments.

Search your reference real estate portal for two-bedroom apartments to rent in a certain area. Then do the same in the same area for three-bedroom apartments. Notice the price difference; it can be around 20% more.

Obviously, if you buy a two-bedroom home and convert it into three, and the renovation is affordable, you can have a very interesting extra profitability.

Well, according to Brandon Turner, the author of the fantastic book "The book on rental property investing", there are around 20% of two-bedroom homes that can be transformed into three-bedroom homes with a little work.

So do the numbers and see if it works out for you. And above all, think about whether you want to manage workers (or do it yourself and dedicate your weekends if you are a handyman).

8.-Homes to be renovated.

Renovations develop your patience like few activities are capable of doing. Apartments to be renovated (and I mean major renovations) can, obviously, generate opportunities.

But the first thing to understand is that from the outset the complexity is much higher and the process is much longer, so the risk is also much greater. In any case, going through it will make you realize that it's not as challenging as it may seem at first glance.

Buying an apartment to renovate is a more complex business because it is actually two businesses in one. In addition to the business of selecting an apartment, negotiating the price, buying the home, selecting a tenant and managing the tenant, a new business is added, which is renovating a home.

In many cases the numbers will only come out if you are successful in managing the reform. And reform is a business, like any other, with its inherent difficulties that mean there are good and bad reformers.

When you want to buy an apartment to renovate, you should expect a high return on your capital (at least double digits). The work you must perform (or outsource) involves inherent risk that should more than compensate you. Therefore, when you do the numbers, you must start earning money significantly from the first day that the apartment is newly renovated.

Once you have renovated the home, its market value should already exceed the total investment you made (purchase + renovation).

Let's look at numbers with a concrete example:

Imagine that a two-bedroom apartment (that does not need renovation) in the neighborhood you are looking at and with similar characteristics has an approximate price of $350,000 (remember to understand the prices well by searching on real estate portals).

If you wanted to buy a home to renovate, the cost of your apartment (with taxes) and the finished renovation (also with the corresponding taxes) should be well below the market price.

Everyone understands that if the apartment plus the renovation cost you $350,000, you have made a bad deal since you have wasted a lot of time and energy along the way to end up paying the same. Remember that when buying an apartment to renovate you are investing:

- TIME: a few months with the money standing still (a complete renovation of a two-bedroom apartment can perfectly take half a year; I know they will tell you four months, but calculate half a year just in case).
- HEADACHES: a lot of management time (although subcontractors remember that maxim that says that in a work you have to be at the top of the canyon every day or at least go overboard very frequently because, if not, the work does not progress at the speed it should).

So how much lower does the price have to be to make it worth it?

It depends on how much you value your price/hour and your

potential headaches. In my current case, with a large family and a job that I am passionate about, but that takes up my time, my price/hour is very high. If I were unemployed my hourly rate would probably drop considerably.

In my opinion, you should be willing to take the risk and aim for a home at least 20% below market value, ideally seeking an even greater discount.

That is, continuing with the example, my opinion is that I would not look for an opportunity where the cost of the apartment and its renovation would cost me more than $280,000.

If we imagine that the apartment has sixty square meters and the renovation costs us about 700 dollars per square meter (it is a standard that varies depending on the condition of the home) and we add some unforeseen events and the corresponding taxes we can quickly find ourselves with renovation costs about $53,000-65,000. This implies that paying more than $185,000 without taxes for the home to be renovated would be risking not earning money for the added value of the renovation.

In conclusion, the price you should aim for when buying a home that needs comprehensive renovation is ideally half the market price after renovation. It is an unscientific rule, but it can help you estimate the maximum prices to pay for an apartment with a major renovation.

Obviously the more expensive the home, the more margin you will have, and then the rule would not work (if you think about homes worth several hundred thousand dollars, the price you could pay is more than half, because in absolute value the renovation will cost you a lot. less).

But since we are focused on apartments for rent and those for less than $350,000 are the ones that generate the greatest added value, as we have seen at the beginning of the book, this "simple rule" can help you not pay more for an apartment that needs to be renovated.

What is the reality of the market?

The reality is that most of the apartments that need to be renovated do not comply with this premise and go on sale for much more expensive than the maximum price you should pay. If you are in a negotiation, explain the reasoning I have told you to the owner. Be transparent with the numbers. Perhaps in this way he understands that the reformer has to earn money for the work he does.

In any case, there are more flats than fish in the sea. Don't get obsessed with any floor. And even less so with apartments that need to be renovated and come with associated headaches. Aspirin costs money and someone has to pay for it.

9.-Apartments that have not been sold for a long time or have just gone on sale.

Sometimes owners make the wrong price when listing an apartment for sale. Normally they make a mistake and put the home up for sale at a higher price than it would have. But on some occasions (few, but it happens) the starting price is below market. On these occasions the fastest wins.

I don't need to tell you that you have to be very agile when this happens. It happened to us in one of our homes and thanks to the alerts from the real estate portals we were able to be the first to visit the home and close the deal. If you know your market well, you will quickly detect these opportunities, because they sing like clams.

"Bargain apartments" require a lot of agility (buying right at the beginning) or a lot of patience (buying much later). The chances of buying an apartment at a very good price increase as time goes by. At the beginning we can take advantage of an incorrect starting price (difficult, but possible) but as time goes by the owners will become nervous and therefore will be more accessible to potential price reductions.

That is why we are going to think about the most common situation. The owner positions an asking price above the market price and the apartment has not been sold for a long time. And when a flat has not been sold for a long time, the same thing always happens. Do you know what happens? What happens is that the owner of that apartment stops receiving calls and visits.

If an apartment is not sold for a long time, it is only for two possible reasons:

1. That floor has a value of zero dollars or a negative value.
2. The sale price of that apartment is incorrect.

Understanding that the most common problem is the second, since the first occurs only in very extraordinary situations (it is an apartment that is located in an area with no rental demand and the recurring costs transform it into a worthless asset, that is, in a liability), we must consider in each case whether the owner will be willing to lower the price or not. And do you know what happens?

When an owner has not received a simple call for nine months, when he receives a new call inquiring about his home, he may be much more open to renegotiating a price that he would not have even considered months or years before. During that time, the owner has been covering all the fixed costs associated with the apartment (taxes, insurance, perhaps mortgage...).

Filter the age of the ad on the real estate portal you use most and try to contact the owner. In some cases, it is difficult to contact older ads and there are usually problems speaking to someone who can explain what is happening with that apartment. Sometimes, when the advertiser is a real estate agency, they may not even bother to contact you after a request for information. So, try to be proactive and call whenever there is a contact number.

I recommend that you avoid starting the call by saying that the price is very expensive and that is why they have not sold the home. They already know that. It took them a while, but they may have finally understood it.

You should openly ask the owner and the agency why the apartment has been on the market for so long. With great humility. From that answer and from questioning and digging a little deeper into the conversation, you can now decide if it is worth visiting or not.

If the apartment is very far from its price, it will be difficult to obtain the necessary reduction so that you can achieve the high profitability you are looking for. In the event that its value is closer to the price, the necessary discount will be lower and therefore the options that you can buy at a good price increase.

Finally, remember that you should not be embarrassed when making an offer. If someone feels offended, that's their problem, not yours. In your case, if you don't feel a little uncomfortable bidding, perhaps it's because you are being too generous.

We are human beings and we like to please others. It's something evolutionary. We are social beings because it was essential for our survival to be so. When you bid on an apartment, you should feel some discomfort. If you want to achieve high profitability, it is possible that the (low) initial offer you present to the owner will stress him out and cause him some discomfort. But sometimes, perhaps the owner reflects and thinks that after all your offer was the first in many months or years.

Remember that you can always say goodbye by saying that, if he is interested later, he can call you back (in fact, this has happened to us recently).

The normal thing is that your offers are not accepted. But remember that to buy an apartment you only need a YES (expect a lot of no's). It's a simple game of probabilities.

Keep in mind that maintaining politeness in your interactions will always benefit you in the long run. You can assertively negotiate on price while maintaining politeness.

10.- Be a "problem solver".

There are countless problems to solve when you want to buy a home.

All the previous cases, which I have already explained to you, are nothing more than solving certain situations. But there are many more in which our ability to solve them will give us extra profitability points:

- Unpleasant odors.
- Dampness with fungi in certain areas of the house.
- Neglected garden and surroundings.
- Very old kitchens and bathrooms (remember that a good kitchen and a good bathroom change the general perception of an apartment).
- Fifty meter apartments with too many tiny rooms that make no sense.
- Very small separate kitchens and dining rooms that can be joined together and become a very nice kitchen-dining room, etc.

When there are obvious problems, 90% of potential buyers avoid them. And it's normal. Problems require your time and management. And your time and management requires extra profitability that you must obtain.

So, if you are a real estate "problem solver", you can obtain extra profitability because you will be able to solve problems that others will not want to solve or will not know about.

The problems are associated with risk. Because sometimes small a priori problems are not so easy to solve.

The quality of an apartment and the relationship with its profitability.

If we compare the floors with Government bonds, very reliable Government bonds (for example, from the US) with very little risk (AAA) and there are junk bonds that give a lot of profitability, but the risk of default is obviously greater.

And the same thing happened with the apartment purchase area. Very good areas with low returns, but very low risk, and, on the contrary. I find it a very interesting simile. But the good thing is that in the case of real estate investment, you control the risk.

That is the key to the risk/return ratio. By being able to control the situation you can greatly reduce the risk. If you have a very clear process for selecting tenants, your probability of non-payment will greatly decrease (even if you are in zone C or rent a low-rent apartment), if you put in place the minimum security and control measures, it will be very difficult Let your home be occupied and so we could continue.

Your management can convert an operation with high profitability and high risk into an operation with high profitability and low/medium risk. Therein lies a large part of the explanation of why your property management skills are so important.

Balancing act: pursuing higher profitability while effectively managing risk.

We have described several ways to either solve problems or select some criteria (without elevator, old, in C zones, with a long time on the market, away from tourist areas or bank property), which will help us gain profitability while our risk increases.

The idea is that you must have an opportunistic mentality and be aware that when you buy an apartment below the market price you are not taking advantage of anyone. You are providing a solution that the seller had not encountered until now.

Obviously by combining several of these strategies you can still gain more profitability. And you may also gain more headaches and more risk.

Even increasing our bank financing if you are able (to 85% or even 90% of the value of the home, sometimes it is possible, but it is not the purpose of this book to explain it) will obviously increase your return on the capital invested. But what about the risk?

The problem with risk is managing it.

If your assets are one hundred times the value of a home in which you assume a lot of risk and the move does not go well, you barely notice it. If the value of your assets is close to zero (or negative) and the move goes wrong, you already know the consequences.

There are people with more or less tendency to risk. That's obvious. What you should think about beyond your profile is in the moment. Your time. Not the market. Market timing cannot be guessed (ever). We don't have a crystal ball. That does not exist. Don't be fooled by false gurus.

What you can understand is your moment. Your professional, personal and patrimonial moment. Your energy and available time. Your motivation, your enthusiasm, your ability to be constant (or not) in your actions and objectives. You should also think about your experience... If you know yourself well and make an effort to try to be objective (obviously something impossible due to the nature of the exercise) you will be able to better understand the risk you are taking in a new investment.

Each investment has a different risk. But the risk always depends on the investor. If my job is to renovate properties, doing a renovation has almost no risk for me. If my job is to provide mortgages, getting a good mortgage has almost no risk for me...

Understand yourself, understand your situation and only then will you understand the risk that you can take in your case at a given moment.

And one last recommendation. Beware of the gratuitous opinions of others (including mine obviously). Listen to everyone (always), but make your own.

What risks exist? What can go wrong? Looking for the area of the good real estate investor. The "good investor" methodology

The harsh reality is that every investment carries some level of risk—none are exempt. If you scratch right, in the end there is always a risk (sometimes the risk is that the state that protects certain assets goes bankrupt, but in the end, there is always a risk).

The good news is that the risk in real estate investment depends a lot on your management.

If we draw a curve between the probability of "terrible things" happening and its relationship with acting in the right way ("being focused on a good management methodology"), we will clearly see how doing things well greatly reduces the probability. that our real estate investments produce negative returns.

Good real estate investor area.

The zone of the good investor is where we should move. There are things that cost almost the same effort to do well as to do them badly. The cost of not selecting a good tenant can be enormous. And the effort in selecting a good tenant is not much greater than not doing so.

The same occurs in the management of repairs or security measures. Our obsession must be to place ourselves in the zone of the good investor, managing with a good method and consistency. It will equate to good returns and low risks.

Once we have highlighted the importance of doing things well, let's analyze the possible risks:

The main risks that we will assume when we invest in a home to rent.

Occupation risk.

The employment rate in the US is low. In general, it is low in all developed countries. Although it is a real problem and it exists. In any case, it is important to understand that it is something possible but unlikely. Especially if you do your homework.

The squatters normally prioritize the homes of banking entities or large holders because they know that it is much easier for them and they generate much less noise in society. So just by investing as a small investor your risk percentage has already dropped drastically.

Additionally, if it really is an issue that is keeping you up at night, you can take additional measures to rest better:

- An alarm.
- Avoid buying low plants.
- Armored door with extra security

Risk of non-payment.

The risk of non-payment is one of the risks I like to talk about the most. I like it because the solutions are relatively easy. There are two options to approach the non-payment problem. My preferred option is the first, although the second lets some investors sleep better.

- **Solution 1:** Select your tenants with a rigorous method by observing data and behaviors. It is for me the best solution. Select your tenants after a good process. In my case I am looking for tenants who can potentially stay for five years or more. Many of our tenants have been in our apartments for a long time. Obviously, you make mistakes with people (sometimes), but if you act rigorously the probability is much lower.

  If the tenant is the right one, it is like when you hire a good professional in a company. Everything is easier. If the tenants stay for five years, they will pay me $105,000 to live in my apartments (on average $1,750 rent). Do you think you shouldn't try to get to know as much as possible someone who should pay you that amount?

  Make numbers of what it costs you not to know your tenants.

Tenant selection is, once you have the asset, the most important process.

Good tenant, few problems. Bad tenant, nightmares for sure. People change everything (for better or worse).

- **Solution 2 : Non-payment insurance.** Magic solution. Cost: 5% of annual rental income. It works quite well because others do the work you should do when selecting the tenant (although in this case they only look at data, not behaviors).

  If you sleep more peacefully, use non-payment insurance. Money is there to use. Get to know yourself and understand if it helps you in this regard.

  But, even if the tenant is solvent, it does not mean that your future relationship with them will be problem-free. Therefore, if you take out non-payment insurance, try to invest time in getting to know the tenant before saying yes.

  If the potential tenant is not charming in the negotiation, over the next few years, things will get complicated.

Risk of repairs.

Every year you will have repairs and different maintenance tasks. Well not every year. But you should save that money because in the long term there will be a part of your budget that will go towards it.

If the apartment is new and you rent it unfurnished, perhaps that percentage will be 3%. If, on the other hand, the apartment is old and full of furniture and appliances, that percentage will perhaps rise to 10% or even slightly more.

Repairs and problem management will exist no matter what. Investing in real estate without addressing problems is akin to aspiring to be a soccer player without enduring challenges. Strength and growth usually come from adversity.

The only thing you can choose is if you want them to be less frequent (new and unfurnished apartments) or more frequent (old and furnished apartments). The latter is more exhausting, but it is also obviously more profitable.

The risk that homes values will decline in the coming years.

In my case I always invest for the long term. At least ten years, but my initial intention is to never sell the properties. We will see how my mentality and priorities evolve after several decades have passed.

It is true that inflation has always existed. And it will continue to exist, although from time to time there have been and will be periods of deflation.

I have no interest in predicting the market, my job, and what should also be yours with this type of investment, is to create assets that generate income (after disbursing 20 or 30% of the value of those assets) that pay for themselves. and on top of that they give me positive cash-flow every month. Final point.

In twenty years, most of my homes will be paid for. And if then the value of the home has risen phenomenally (it is the most likely scenario). And if the value of the home has gone down, then that's also great because it will surely have allowed me to buy more and better homes during these twenty years.

When you look at the very long term, market declines three or five years from now seem like anecdotes that you should keep to yourself to tell your grandchildren.

How would I start to act if I had to buy my first high-yield home?

Salespeople who sell apartments like to sell a $700,000 home much more than a $140,000 home. You can imagine the reason, right?

The commission they generate with a more expensive sale is much higher and the work is often similar or less, since the discounts necessary to invest in apartments of $140,000 are not easy to obtain.

If I were starting out, in addition to obviously making a living through alerts of new apartments on the most important real estate portals, I would try to resort to the help of the best real estate agents.

The profession of real estate agent does not have a very good reputation. Although the general level is low and the practices, they use are not always the most ethical, there are good real estate agents. Especially those that have been around for a long time and that have been able to overcome serious economic crises where sales suffer drops of more than 50% or even come to a standstill for long periods.

If you want to contact a good real estate agent, I recommend that you visit three to five real estate agencies that have been in your area for a long time (forget about those agencies that have emerged in recent years of real estate boom).

Tell them that you are going to invest in an apartment for $140,000-2300,000 (or whatever budget you have in your head) and the profitability criteria you need for this particular investment. You can tell them that in addition to the commission they will take from the seller, you are willing to pay them a few more percentage points or an extra fixed amount (2,000, 3,000, 4,000 dollars?) so that they really see that you are serious. Obviously, it fulfills your commitment if you buy an apartment through them with the clear criteria that you have set for them.

Real estate agents are motivated by incentives. Let them see that their work will be rewarded. And show them that you can help generate additional income. One last recommendation. If you find a good real estate agent. Take care of it a lot! It is a treasure. If the agent is good and you are a serious investor, he will continually feed you with opportunities (potential deals, the famous deal flow).

Remember that you get the extra profitability mainly from the purchase price you obtain. So be patient. Have a working method and don't be ashamed to make low offers. The normal thing is that out of every ten or fifteen offers, maybe one will be accepted. As I have already told you, if they accept offers in a higher proportion, perhaps you are being too generous in your price.

Did you think that generating profitability would be easier?

Is not easy. And it requires time and knowledge. But it's worth it. Constantly learn and repeat the process over and over again if you feel comfortable. And finally, I show you a real case with numbers so that you finish reading the chapter with that extra motivation that pushes you to act.

The numbers of a real estate investment that have generated 12.4% annually for me for four years.

This is a studio in the center of the city. It is a third floor with an elevator, already renovated, for which they were asking $135,000. Amount that I finally ended up paying. I bought it five minutes after visiting. It was a "bargain apartment." And we acted very quickly.

We could use many different ratios or KPIs to calculate the profitability of the operation. But let's go to the simplest ones.

First of all, let's calculate the cash flow of the operation.

To do this, we will have to calculate all the income that the home generates for us in a year. And likewise, all the expenses.

Annual cash flow= annual income - annual expenses.

Let's start by calculating the income:

- In this case the current rent is $1,165.
- $1,165 x 12 months = $13,980 annual income.

Regarding recurring housing expenses.

- The monthly mortgage payment: In this home, 75% of the total amount was financed over twenty-five years with a fixed rate of 2%. Therefore, the resulting mortgage payment is $438. Annually it is 5,256 dollars.
- Community fees: $70 monthly, $838 annually.
- Home insurance: $279 annually.
- Life insurance (associated with the mortgage): $350 annually.
- Real estate tax: $466 annually.
- Maintenance expenses, we could indicate 10% (although it has been lower): $1,400 annually.
- We will allocate 5% of the time as a standard measure of unoccupied housing time (although it has been less): $700.
- The sum of all annual expenses = $9,309.
-

And, therefore, the annual cash flow will be: income - expenses = 13,980 – 9,309 = $4,671.

You would have to subtract from this amount other taxes that you pay depending on your country or region. In our case, approximately $3,400 will ultimately remain.

Therefore, from these analyzes we can now analyze some profitability ratios:

The gross profitability of the operation (total annual income/total housing cost with taxes) = 13,980/ 135,000 = 10.3%.

This is a measure that I use a lot to quickly rule out homes that I know will not have a good return. In cases of gross returns above 6% I know that (with the current financing conditions) the operation will generate positive cash flow without problems and also obviously the home will pay for itself.

One of the most used ratios is the return on money invested

(ROCE). In this home we have seen that the cash-flow it generates for us annually is 3,400 dollars. On the other hand, we put in $52,750 of equity capital.

Therefore, the ROCE (or return on capital equity) is 3,400/52,750 = 6.4%.

So, this investment has required us to disburse $52,750 and returns us $3,400 each year in money that enters our pocket (already deducted from taxes).

For investors who are exclusively dedicated to investing in rental housing, this is a critical measure. Probably the most important one for them.

Why?

This is because it represents the only money flowing into their pockets month after month. For example, if someone wanted to have an income of $3,500 per month through this type of investment, they would need to buy 11.6 (twelve) apartments like the one we have seen in the example. $3,400 monthly x 12 months / $3,500 = 11.65.

Is that the only profitability that this investment brings us? Without a doubt, not!

There are other very important returns that we must take into account as I have already mentioned at the beginning of the book. With each passing month, in addition to putting money in our pockets, mortgage debt decreases. In this case, during the first year the debt amortization payment amounts to $5,256. Of the 438 dollars per month, around 265 go to amortized capital and 173 to interest.

Furthermore, each year this amortized amount increases, meaning that more interest is paid at the beginning of the period than at the end.

We consider these $5,256 of less debt that we have left at the end of the year as an extra return. And with respect to our initial outlay, this extra annual return is 3,180/52,750 = 6%.

So, to the 6.4% return on cash flow, we should add the 6% return on amortization of the mortgage debt that pays itself through rent payments.

The profitability is now 12.4% (cash flow + debt reduction).

But, in addition, when buying a home, we are buying an asset. And we know that assets tend to appreciate over time due to inflation. Which in this case we will not take into account for the calculations.

And if you also initially buy an apartment below the market price (as is surely what happened in this case and you already start with an extra initial profitability) you might think that you can reach returns close to 20% annually for ten years.

One last note. Don't let profitability blind you. And don't let it obsess you either. Perhaps you believe that the proposed maintenance costs (10% of income) are too high and the real profitability is higher or perhaps you think the opposite. The same with the time scenarios of the empty home (which by the way depends a lot on your management) or with the inflation estimates. It doesn't matter too much. Because the reality is that double-digit profitability year after year is not normal or common in many investments. But as you have seen in the case of real estate investments in certain types of homes, it is achievable (with its associated risks).

This high profitability is a result of your efforts in searching for, and importantly, eliminating homes, as well as in their professional management.

We have other less profitable apartments as well. Apartments that give us peace of mind. Apartments that may be a future home for our daughters. Apartments that may give us future liquidity if we needed to sell them due to unforeseen events (life, as you know, is full of surprises).

Learning is what transforms the world. And learning is what can perhaps make you a great real estate investor.

CHAPTER 5 - FINANCIAL STRATEGIES TO BOOST YOUR INVESTMENTS: DISCOVER THE KEYS TO OBTAINING THE BEST FINANCING AND SCALING YOUR BUSINESS

When a promising investment is within reach, financing typically becomes a manageable challenge. There are multiple ways to finance our real estate investments. The most important thing is that you understand that the first thing is always that "the operation" makes sense and the mathematics adds up. If the numbers add up, we will have to analyze, based on our situation, what is the best way to finance these operations.

While there are numerous ways to finance real estate investments, below is a list that I will delve into shortly:

- Mortgage loan.
- FF (Family and Friends).
- Cash.
- Second mortgage.
- Pledged shares or funds.
- Personal bank loan.
- Room rental.
- Seller loan subrogation.
- Partnerships.

Ten ways to finance a real estate transaction.

I am pretty clear about my recommendations when it comes to

financing my own real estate operations. The lifetime mortgage is my favorite. In any case, for some people who cannot qualify for a mortgage, there are also other options that are worth analyzing and that can also work if executed correctly.

1.- Mortgage loan.

A mortgage loan is probably the most common way to buy your first home as an investment. It undoubtedly has many advantages: long-term credit, low interest rates or the possibility of requesting credit at a fixed or variable rate.

There are many entities that offer this service and since there is so much competition, the options for the consumer are usually very varied and really competitive.

The most effective way to get the best possible financing is to have several financing offers. So direct and so simple. But so, few people apply. In any negotiation, the key to determining your position is to be ready to walk away when you have a better alternative.

So, in any negotiation, the first person you have to convince is yourself. Do not forget.

How to negotiate a mortgage well?

Financing is crucial as the profitability, and thus the sustainability, of your real estate investments hinges on two fundamental factors:

1. Your ability to find profitable investments.
2. Your ability to keep the cost of money as low as possible.

Prior to the onset of the COVID-19 pandemic, interest rates had remained low for an extended period, enabling individuals to secure mortgages with interest rates below 3%, either at a fixed or variable rate. Currently, after a period of negative interest rates, central banks have raised interest rates due to the problem of inflation, but it is a situation that will not last forever and in any case the price of housing is also affected by the interest rates.

Historically, if interest rates rise, the price of housing tends to fall (or rise less than it did previously) because financing them is more expensive. And the opposite effect should also occur.

In any case, although the mortgage interest rate is one of the most important variables in the price of housing, it is not the only one. The price of housing depends on many other factors such as: the occupancy rate, the migratory flow or GDP growth, among others.

Whether interest rates are more or less high, any reduction in financing costs will be direct additional profitability injected into the vein. To negotiate effectively, consider gathering ample information. For instance, use online mortgage comparators to obtain an initial understanding.

With these comparators we can obtain quite competitive conditions in fifteen minutes (we simply have to fill out a form) which will then allow us to go to the bank and allow us to start the negotiation from a stronger and more informed position. It is especially important that the bank manager understands that we have moved and that if he wants our mortgage business, he will have to make an effort and we offer conditions that are far from the standard (and usually more expensive) rates of the entity.

All banking entities want good customers (current or potential) and are willing to make efforts (lower margins) to get them.

When I talk to real estate investors, one of the comments they repeat the most is that they regret the poor mortgage conditions they obtained in their first investments. With the knowledge they have accumulated over the years they would be able to achieve much better conditions. It is normal. It can happen to all of us. However, now you are aware.

It is likely that you have had the mortgage for ten, fifteen, twenty or even thirty years, so it is worth working on the financing in advance and, above all, playing your cards well: even if you do not have much assets or a very high income, it can be a lot. better than you think a priori.

Smart managers want investing clients. They are the ones that end up generating the most income for the bank. But it is also true that the risk profile of a novice investor is higher than that of a buyer of their usual home. Therefore, it is also important that the manager knows you well and understands your way of acting, your values, your education. When in doubt, your behavior will certainly make a difference. As in so many other things in life, the HOW is as important or more important than the WHAT.

For the first floor, financing through a mortgage is in most cases the best way to finance. It has many advantages for the consumer. The law has greatly protected it from abusive clauses and most of the additional costs and taxes must be paid by the banking entity (but obviously it ends up being assumed by the client with a usually higher opening commission or a higher interest rate).

In the event that 100% financing is extraordinarily needed.

In principle, it is not advisable to increase the risk unless you have a good emergency fund. You can also extend mortgages to forty years. You can use to negotiate the services of mortgage brokers who will charge you an extra commission if you work with them (maximum by law of 5% of the mortgage amount, although the normal thing is that their commission varies from 2 to 4% depending on the type of service you hire).

Online brokers will accompany you in the process and therefore may also be interesting for those who have less time. Although remember that they will charge you for this service.

Fixed rate or variable rate mortgage?

Regarding the big question about whether to choose a fixed-rate or variable-rate mortgage: there is no single correct answer.

Some reflections that I always transmit:

- Only as the years go by will you know if you have minimized your interest payments or not.
- Remember that more interest is paid at the beginning than at the end (even if the installment remains the same).
- If you use a fixed rate, you reduce an uncertainty in the rental business (the cost of financing) in exchange (obviously) for a higher price (at least in the first years).
- Think about whether you have enough cash (or not) to withstand a hypothetical increase in interest rates. If you can bear it (for example, amortizing) perhaps a variable rate is better for you, if you can't, perhaps a fixed rate. Be careful with this exercise: humans are terrible at making predictions of our needs 3-5 years ahead, imagine ten or fifteen years ahead!

In short, the mortgage loan is probably the best option for you to get started in the exciting world of real estate investment. But, as I have told you, invest time, acquire information and negotiate hard.

Ah! And remember: solid financing won't rescue a poor investment, but inadequate financing can jeopardize a promising one.

2.- Partnerships.

I have carried out all the real estate transactions with a partner. In my case, my wife. If we had not carried out the operations jointly, the reality is that the financing conditions would probably have been worse and we probably would not have been able to carry out the same number of operations.

As you can imagine, making investments with partners is something that should not be taken lightly. Although it has important advantages (because as they say, "with company you can always go further than alone") it is very important to choose the right partners. A mistake in choosing a partner is very expensive (both from an emotional and financial point of view).

When we talk about buy&hold type real estate investments (buying apartments to rent) the investments are for very long periods of time (dozens of years on many occasions). It's hard to know if you and your potential partners will have the same interests in fifteen years. Because priorities in life change. For all. Therefore, when making a partnership it is always very important to make a partners' agreement (in writing) where it is very clear how the partnership will end.

Rest assured that sooner or later, every partnership comes to an end. Obviously, there are no eternal ones. If it lasts long, death is what ends it. If your partner is your partner, probably the partners' agreement is your marriage (and the type of matrimonial property regime you signed). But if this is not the case, remember to write and sign that partners' agreement that includes the different causes of dissolution of the partnership and the consequences of each of them. Obviously consult with a lawyer to draft the documents thoroughly and legally at the same time.

3.- Personal bank loan.

A bank loan can help us complement part of the down payment that we must face when investing in a home. It is also an interesting option for when we have to tackle a major renovation and we do not have enough cash.

In any case, my recommendation is that the real estate operation has a very good profitability since it will be the only way to compensate for the high bank interest to be paid for the personal loan.

The advantages of a personal loan are quite evident. It is a relatively easy option to obtain and quick since there is no mortgage guarantee that supports it. The problem is that the interest is much higher than mortgage interest. They can be 3 to 7 percentage points higher and, in addition, the maximum amounts are usually capped at around $60,000.

The maximum repayment period is around 5-7 years, so depending on the amount we ask for, we may find ourselves with a high monthly payment that we will have to face. Be careful. Think carefully about all the options you have before requesting a personal loan

4.- Second mortgages.

A financing method that you can use if you already own a home is to take out a second mortgage on that home to pay for the new one. his way, you would acquire a new apartment while retaining ownership of the previous one, which could be rented out.

Therefore, if you already have an apartment and its value is much higher than the pending amount of your mortgage, you have an additional source of financing that you can use to invest in a new property.

5.- FF (Family and Friends).

A recurring option is to go to family (or even friends, although if a friend leaves you money to buy a home, they may not fully understand what they are doing). With this source of financing, your family could guarantee a mortgage loan, allowing the bank to finally approve your credit. Alternatively, they could also provide you with money in the form of a loan.

In the case of the bank guarantee, remember that if you do not pay, it is the family member who is responsible with their current or future assets. As you can imagine, being a guarantor entails significant and serious consequences if things do not go well. It is an option that, beyond the most direct blood lines (parents-children), I see as quite risky and, in my opinion, should be avoided whenever possible to avoid misunderstandings.

Family (or friends) could also provide you with a personal loan for a specific temporary period. In such cases, I recommend documenting the loan in writing and notifying the tax authorities to avoid it being classified as a concealed donation.

The legal document of the loan should be very clear about the exact amount of the loan, the interest rate applied (it should be with market rates), the loan repayment periods and even what happens in case of non-repayment of the loan. . It is important to repay the loan with bank transfers (so that we can demonstrate that the loan has been repaid if necessary).

There is only one family. Yourself. Treat you well. And friends the same, don't turn them into enemies.

6.- Subrogation of the seller's loans.

You should know that in some cases when you buy a home it is possible to continue with the mortgage that the seller had on the asset you buy, subrogating you to the mortgage debt. It is commonly an option in real estate purchases to assume the developer's mortgage. But it is not the only case in which it is possible to do so.

It is worth understanding if there is a mortgage associated with the property you buy and if the conditions are better than what you could get, try to subrogate that mortgage. Obviously, the bank must accept this subrogation with the consequent risk analysis, but, if possible, you can obtain financing at very good conditions.

7.- Rent rooms in the habitual residence or rent the vacation home.

One of the richest people I know, with assets of over $250 million, has wonderful summer homes in different areas. There are at least two areas where I know he has second and third dream properties. They tend to be old farmhouses or farms restored down to the smallest detail.

The best of all is that maintaining these restored properties does not cost the owner a penny. And they are always in magazines. As it does? As you can imagine the owner rents his residences when he does not need them. In addition, he views his residence as just another business than he already has.

It is curious that a person with hundreds of millions of dollars of assets rents their vacation homes without any problem and that there are many owners who would not rent their second home under any circumstances even though they use it less than thirty days a year.

I respect all opinions. It would be missing more. But on many occasions, due to this reason, many owners have to end up selling their second home, because they cannot maintain it. Or worse still, they have second homes with little maintenance and therefore during their vacations they find themselves in uncomfortable places (being hot or cold) because they cannot invest in having the properties in optimal condition.

Life already comes with its share of challenges; owning a second residence that we rarely enjoy and that also incurs costs can add unnecessary complications. Right now, you might ask yourself: why am I explaining this story to you in the middle of a real estate financing chapter?

The answer is that when you buy a home and see it as an asset and want to generate profitability with it, there are many creative ways that can help you finance that home. Regardless of whether you use a mortgage or a private loan, the way you pay those loans monthly can come from different sources of income.

Thus, an option that some use to buy their first home to rent is to buy a home to live in and at the same time also use it to rent.

In many cases, in this way, tenants finance the home they live in and begin to learn about the property rental business.

There are many ways to rent homes to help you finance them:

- Some buy a three- or four-bedroom home and rent out the rooms they don't use.
- Others rent the house where they live completely only during holiday periods with strong demand and high prices (and during those periods they look to live in other houses of family or friends).
- Others even buy houses that they prepare and segregate into two and permanently rent one of the two parts.

- Or others buy a second home for their vacations and it turns out that the temporary rentals they make when they are not using it cover all the costs of the home and still generate profitability.

There are many ways to rent your own asset. Without a doubt, it can be a way to gain confidence and experience in the property rental business.

8.- Pledged other assets (for investors with assets through private banking).

The next form of financing is usually reserved for clients with a certain amount of assets. The so-called clients with assets exceeding $1,00,000 who act with private banking managers. Normally, most large banks segment their clients based on their current or potential assets to provide more personalized services to their best clients.

Pledge is one of those services that is usually only available to private banking clients. For this reason, the conditions of a pledged credit are negotiated in a very individualized manner depending on the client's profile.

Pledge consists of immobilizing monetary assets as collateral, such as money, shares, investment funds or fixed-income securities such as promissory notes or treasury bills to obtain a percentage of financing on the amount that is immobilized.

Pledge loans are uncommon and often unfamiliar to many. Although mortgage credit is granted with the guarantee of real estate, pledging a loan involves leaving a financial asset as a "pledge" or as collateral, such as shares, shares in funds, deposits or insurance.

The great advantage for the client is that, although during the duration of the loan the pledged asset remains unavailable, they can continue to enjoy the profitability it generates. If a share pays a dividend, the client collects it, but cannot sell the shares except to repay the credit.

9.- Loans from private investment networks.

This line of financing is usually unknown, although it is much more common than people think (especially among the investment community).

What happens when you do not meet the usual conditions that banks ask for to obtain financing?

Some investors give up continuing to invest in real estate, while others resort to private loans from investment networks. So that you can see some real examples of the reasons and conditions under which several of these private loans are made, I have gone to a professional lender with a good reputation to find out the details of the operations it offers.

I attach some examples below so you can understand how they work:

Some examples of private loan conditions with mortgage guarantees:

Example 1- Financial conditions

- Maximum principal: $2,100,000.
- Net opening commission for the investor: 1.00%.
- Ordinary interest: 12.50%.
- Default interest: 14.00%.
- Term: 12 months (with the possibility of extending by 6 more months. Renewal commission: 1.00%).
- Liquidity for the investor (the one who puts in the money): monthly.
- Mortgage guarantees and additional guarantees: Two single-family homes are mortgaged in high-value tourist areas, both very exclusive and with extremely high-quality finishes. The financing is granted to a company. The Loan-to-value (LTV) is 28%, but the client also personally guarantees the operation.
- Client profile and project viability: This is a group of

companies. The money will be used for the imminent works on one of its commercial assets. They will repay the loan directly from the benefits generated by their regular activity. In addition, the client owns real estate assets and has put two assets in his real estate portfolio up for sale.

Example #2- Financial conditions

- Maximum principal: $2,300,000
- Opening fee: 1.00%
- Ordinary interest rate: 12.90%
- Term: 12 months
- Investor liquidity: monthly
- LTV:33.50%
- Personal endorsement: Yes (both from the father and the daughter, who is the sole administrator of the company).
- Purpose of the loan: professional investments.
- Mortgage and additional guarantees: the client is the owner of a property, as well as eight other assets. -residential and commercial-. The property is mortgaged in a preferential range (maximum mortgage on the existing first mortgage so that investors are in first effective charge). The financing is granted to the company holding the asset. The final LTV counting all charges is 33%, and also has the additional guarantee of the personal guarantee of both the father and the daughter (sole administrator of the company).
- Client profile and project viability: business client specialized in the textile sector. The capital will be used for the company's productive internationalization. The financing will be resolved with the sale of the asset that is already in the marketing process.

As evident, these are short-term loans (lasting months or a few years) secured by a mortgage (requiring some form of asset). These are loans that some real estate investors use when, for example, they buy a property that needs renovation. It is much more difficult to obtain regular bank financing for properties with a very important renovation, since banks are more reluctant to finance this type of operation (because if there are problems and they have to keep the property, they know that the liquidity of a property to be renovated is much smaller).

Therefore, some investors opt for private loans to finance property acquisitions, conduct renovations, and subsequently rent out the homes. Once the home is in perfect condition, they take out a mortgage loan with a financial institution, pay the private loan and liquidate the mortgage guarantee associated with the loan.

They are special operations that usually do not make much sense when carrying out the first real estate operation, but it is important that you know their existence in case your plan is to achieve a significant number of real estate assets.

The interest rates are usually quite high (to attract investors who are the ones who lend the money), but obtaining the loan is quite quick if you meet the conditions and have assets that can guarantee the operation.

10.- Cash (cash payment).

A good friend of mine, a manager, has his habitual residence paid for and a house, which he inherited, in an idyllic environment. As he accumulated capital in the form of reserves, he didn't quite know what to do with the several hundred thousand dollars he had accumulating in his accounts.

For this reason, he decided to invest in a home to rent, paying the total price of the home (and the corresponding taxes) in cash. He bought a practically new small two-bedroom home. The final net tax-free return he obtains is below 3%. It is a low profitability, but it seems good to him when he compares it with the non-existent profitability of bank accounts or with the ups and downs that he cannot digest well in variable income.

His investment philosophy is grounded in the belief that avoiding debt makes it nearly impossible to go bankrupt. And without a doubt he is very right about that. And you know what? I think it's great (although I prefer to use debt to accelerate our assets). He is happy and calm and that has been his way of buying his first home as an investment. He can pay in cash because he has the money and gives up having more profitability (he could buy several homes with the money with which he bought one if he leveraged himself) to gain peace of mind.

Paying with cash is a possibility. And you should know that it exists. And there are some investors who use it. And may everyone be happy with their decisions. Of course!

While my primary recommendation is the mortgage route, there are instances where combining multiple financing sources can be beneficial in securing the required funds for the operation.

Conclusion about the importance of financing.

The real estate business is based on a very simple premise. The recurring financing costs and all associated costs of the asset must be less than the recurring income that the asset provides us. When the previous point is met, the operation has a positive profitability and therefore with each month that passes there is more money in our pocket. For this reason, understanding how we finance an operation is half of the equation. The other half is understanding income.

Financing is the half that depends most on you. You choose through which sources you borrow, with what periods and even if you repay your debt in advance or not.

Information is power. And in this aspect, a power that will make you pay much less interest.

Remember: There is no good financing that can save a bad investment, but there is bad financing that can ruin a good operation.

CHAPTER 6 - MASTERING THE PSYCHOLOGY OF BUYERS AND SELLERS: EFFECTIVE STRATEGIES FOR NEGOTIATING HOME PRICES

There are negotiations that can have a high impact on our lives. Negotiating a salary increase or successfully negotiate a significant reduction in the purchase of a home has a very important impact on our finances.

In this chapter, I analyze how to maximize our chances of obtaining a significant discount on the purchase of a home, whether for investment purposes or even for personal residence.

The psychology of the buyer: a correct mindset and control of your emotions.

It will not always be possible to get a discount on a home. In fact, the normal thing is not to get it. It's essentially a game of probabilities. So, the first thing is to prepare the negotiation with a good mentality and understand that, if we are going to negotiate with a strong, calm, and, most importantly, prepared mindset, our probability increases.

We all watch a lot of movies. It is normal. We like stories. And normally the movie negotiator is painted as a serious man, with huge jaws and a poker face.

Make no mistake. To negotiate, these types of attitudes cause the opposite effect to what we are looking for. So, if you aim for successful negotiations, being amicable is far more effective than appearing emotionless like a machine. Although I already tell you that just with your kindness you will not get a discount from the seller.

A method is needed. A method that guides you and allows you to control your emotions. There are many types of home buyers:

- There are those who accept practically everything the seller asks of them. And they also thank them for "letting them buy the home."
- At the other extreme, there are people who haggle over everything and who have lost negotiations because they want to be radical and win every last cent.

The process of negotiating the price of a home is absolutely conditioned by emotions. Both on the buying side and on the selling side. Therefore, the key to obtaining the best price is controlling your emotions and good planning (being very clear about your financial details and following a reliable method to negotiate and maximize your options).

Next, I will show you in detail the method that has allowed me to reach good agreements for both parties (the buyer and the seller) in different home buying and selling processes that I have experienced. But before going into the details of the method, the psychology of the seller is also important.

Salesperson psychology is usually very subjective.

If you put yourself in the seller's shoes you will understand much better what your behavior as a buyer should be. To begin with, the seller is a person just like you, with all that comes with it.

The seller has expectations (real or unreal), he has feelings about the home (or not) and he has needs (most of them irrational, like almost all human needs today in developed countries.

If the seller could sell the home for twice as much, he would do so. Obviously. If the seller could choose who to sell the home to from a queue of potential buyers, he would choose according to his criteria (perhaps the one who pays the fastest, perhaps the one he likes best, perhaps the one who takes better care of his beloved home...). We do not know. It is difficult to understand the salesperson's millions of neural circuits.

And sellers typically list their homes for sale in a manner similar to how you would post a new photo on Instagram. He clicks on the current real estate portal (alone or with the help of a real estate agent) and hopes that thousands of people will tell him how wonderful his home is and "take it off his hands."

And then, almost always, you barely receive a message or call and little else. And that human being who plays the role of the salesperson can have very different reactions to that first disappointment.

A classic one is the following: "Whoever sees my house, keeps it. The value cannot be seen in the photos. But when he sees her in person everything will change." And so, we could continue filling in phrases associated with the seller's usual psychology.

And the buyer? That's you. And you want to get a home below market price, right? If so, first, you must understand the size of that market you want to take a bite out of, so the first question you should ask yourself is: How many below-market homes are sold in your target area? How often does a home in your area sell for below market price?

Most houses in your region were obviously sold at market price. In fact, that is the definition of market price. The rational and usual selling price of a certain asset. But you will agree, if you know the famous Gauss curve, we will find at the beginning of the curve a series of sold homes that will undoubtedly be at a lower or much lower price than they should be and vice versa.

This occurs by pure chance 5% of the time (more or less when we deviate more than two times the standard deviation from the mean). So, if you live in a populated area, it's likely that every day or two (or at least weekly) homes near your area are selling below market price.

Is the seller ready to sell at a discount?

You will not be able to buy a home with a significant discount from a person who is not prepared.

To sell their home at a below market price, a seller must either:

- Understand and accept certain reasoning.
- Not having any idea what the market price is.

Psychology plays a fundamental role in the sale (and purchase) of a home. Therefore, on many occasions events must occur for a seller to be prepared to sell at a discount. The most common thing is that time (or a lot of time) must pass in which the seller does not receive offers for his mentality to gradually change.

Accepting that your home is not worth what the seller thinks it is worth is a process, never an event.

In any case, just because the seller is not completely closed does not mean that it will be easy to convince him. And that's where the method comes into play. It's when we should do everything, we can to ensure that, if the seller is open to changing their point of view, we maximize the chances of securing a better deal.

And it all starts with understanding the main motivation for the sale.

The method to aspire to buy homes below the market price.

1.- Why is the home for sale?

In many cases the reason for selling a home is not so obvious. And the seller usually hides it. Obviously, if he needs to sell quickly, he is not used to telling you: "I am desperate, in debt and I need you to buy my house at whatever price." This normally does not happen. Normal, right?

Understanding why the seller is selling the home is much more important than you can imagine. And many times, to obtain that information the only way is through indirect questions:

- Are you going to buy a bigger home then?
- Are you staying in the neighborhood?
- Does your work take you too far?

In the end, the issue is not that important. The important thing is to ask openly so that the seller can talk. Sometimes the seller will take a while to open up and therefore we will have to try different open questions at different stages of the first visit.

Some common reasons to sell a house:

- Job change.
- Liquidity need.
- Search for homes with better characteristics (terrace, light, height...).
- Same as in the previous case, but doing a downgrading (too old to grow old, to move to a better area, to be close to a child...).
- A relationship breaks down and the home has to be sold to close the stage.
- An inheritance that must be distributed among family members.
- A bank home.

There are many more reasons, but ultimately, understanding the motivation will enable us to grasp two fundamental variables better:

- The urgency or non-urgency to sell (time).
- Price sensitivity (dividing a home among ten owners is not the same as dividing it between two, as we have already seen in a previous chapter. Or having to settle a debt with a very high amount is not the same as having to settle it with a low compared to the value of the home.

2.- Is the initial price of the home at a correct market price?

It seems evident that the homes that are worst positioned in price with respect to "their real value" are the homes for which we should be able to negotiate stronger discounts from the start, right? After all, they are very separate from the real value. My experience tells me that this is usually not the case. I think the reason is easy to understand.

When a home goes on sale at a low price, it is because the seller has not done his job and has not looked (or has not wanted to see) what his home is worth at the market price.

This happens a lot. In fact, homes on average end up being sold at a significant discount compared to the price at which they initially appear on the platforms. It seems that, on average, potential home buyers are willing to pay 20% less than the initial published price. The final reality is that (on average) operations end up closing at a midpoint between the portal's offer and what is offered by the client.

Why do many sellers have temporary blindness with the price of their home?

Many sellers define the price based on reasoning that does not set the price but rather according to personal reasoning that the potential buyer is not interested in.

Typical incorrect reasoning when setting the price by the seller:

- The house cost me X dollars Z years ago.
- I need to sell for Y dollars to be able to buy the new home I want.
- The debt I have left is Z dollars.
- The neighbor is selling his for XX dollars (it's been on sale for four years, by the way). So, mine, which has three more square meters and a very nice lamp, is worth XX + 10% dollars.
- Look what beautiful paint I've put on the floor. It is ivory in color.

They are typical limiting beliefs of the salesperson. And I assure you that in general there is only one way to overcome those beliefs. The way is the indifference of the market for a good period of time. Therefore, when a new home is out of position in price, I recommend that you stay away from it. It will be very difficult to convince the seller (who has not been able to do a minimum of rational research) to sell it to you at a very significant discount.

You can put these dispositioned homes on the radar only when several months (or years) have passed. A home initially priced too high can turn into a good opportunity as months or years pass without market attention.

3.- What rational reasons can we use to reduce an a priori fair price?

Let's think that there is a home that goes on sale with a "fair price." How could we get an additional that allows us to save thousands or tens of thousands of dollars? What arguments can we use? When one wants to argue about a price it is necessary to look for a support point.

If the argument you give to the seller is that there are two homes just like yours (imagine that it is a promotion with several homes for sale) that sell 10% cheaper, the seller cannot give you a solid answer beyond tell you that his microwave is "Smegg" brand and that it cost him $580. There you have a strong negotiating foothold.

On the other hand, if your support point is that you don't like the color of the floor and that is why you are going to need to change it and invest $7,000 in a new floor, your negotiation support point is very weak.

Seeking strong and (practically) indisputable support points is the 'most crucial rational strategy' you will employ to negotiate a price reduction with the selling party.

What are the most common anchors that will help you negotiate a discount when purchasing a home?

- Market benchmarking is basic. Understand what similar opportunities there are in the area. and at what prices. If you are an investor and invest frequently, do not hesitate to show evidence to the selling party regarding the price at which you have purchased similar homes (obviously only if the information is true and the prices are lower).

- If you are an investor and are looking for a certain profitability, show the profitability calculation document directly (please keep it simple) and if you have other homes that meet that profitability criterion, show the numbers of those other homes to the seller as well.

- Your argument is very clear and simple. "I need a X% gross profitability, if I can't get it with this home, I will have to look for it through other opportunities."

- Discuss the renovation costs that you will have to assume if you have to change some basic facilities such as bathrooms, the kitchen or the electrical installation. To help you in this aspect you should know that some of the most common renovation costs are:

  o Complete renovation of a home: starting at about $600 per square meter (obviously you can spend as much as you want). A home of about one hundred square meters that you must completely renovate will rarely cost less than $60,000.

  o Bathroom and kitchen renovation: this is a fairly common renovation. The average price could be around $300-370 per square meter. Normally a complete kitchen does not cost less than $10,000 and each bathroom has at least $7,000 in labor and materials costs.

○ Painting a home: from $700 to $3,500 (obviously depending on the size).

○ Change the entire electrical installation: starting at about $5,500.

4.- It's not just the price. You must consider other concepts.

Walking is a great activity. It gives us mental freshness and helps us solve many problems in our daily lives. The same thing happens when you negotiate. Sometimes it's good to walk. What do I mean?

You should not focus the negotiation only on the price. Yes, it is the most important factor, but it is not the only one. There are many concepts to negotiate.

If we find ourselves completely stuck on the issue of price, we can agree on other terms to foster greater empathy and create a sense of progress in the negotiation. Then, once we have "moved forward" we will renegotiate the price again.

What are the common elements, beyond price, that you can negotiate?

• A high and quick deposit to generate confidence that we will close the operation and we have not come to make things worse.

• The extra payment for furniture that the seller doesn't know what to do with and that we may end up throwing away later (offering $100,000 for a home is not the same as offering $95,000 + $5,000 for the furniture).

• Yes, for the buyer it is the same. But for the seller it is not. Sometimes, it can work. I assure you. This is because we empathize with the value that the seller attributes to his furniture (yes, I know, forty-year-old furniture that you won't be able to get by selling). Think about how the seller thinks. If you are selfish, think of others. You will do better.

- Unusual transaction closing deadlines. If you buy affordable homes, you may be able to pay for them in cash directly. And you can save the seller the "tedious" two to three months typical of paperwork and processes with the notary. If you can offer a sale in a few days and not in a few months, you have a very powerful weapon.

- Negotiate special needs of the seller. Imagine that the seller needs a few months to look for a new home to live in (whether renting or buying). Why don't you give him complete flexibility to take the time he needs? Perhaps by making an earnest money contract with a much longer expiration date than usual. Or perhaps the opposite happens. Listen to the seller and observe and investigate what he really needs and offer him everything that is not a big problem for you, but that makes the seller's life enormously easier.

When you walk, your vision of the situation changes. We have all experienced it. Walk with the seller beyond the price. And once you have made progress, return to the issue of price. By then, you will have already reached a preliminary agreement on something. And you will surely be closer to closing a potential agreement.

5.- The power and importance of time and putting the odds in your favor.

Hello good morning! My name is Albert. I'm going to buy his apartment for $180,000. Yes, the one he advertises for $260,000. If he wants, next week we will sign the sale. Calm!

Negotiating a discount is not a task similar to that of preparing instant coffee. You will need days, meetings, moments, reflections, negative responses... And the normal thing is that in the end you will not get the price. But if you engage consistently in negotiations across various opportunities, you will end up saving thousands of dollars and getting much higher returns.

You won't have achieved it by being very clever. You will simply have achieved it because the probabilities, in the end, will have allied themselves with your methodical and persevering way of working. It is very difficult that after making dozens of downward offers you cannot get a yes.

What I can assure you is that it is IMPOSSIBLE to obtain a YES if you have not made any offer. It is an irrefutable axiom. And when you achieve it, I assure you that few activities in your life will have brought you a better profit/hour than a good negotiation in the purchase of a home.

6.- How to present a downward offer?

The negotiation process may bear some resemblance to the process of dating a new partner. Although each couple is different, there are usually some common phases that you should know.

Never send an offer the same day you visit a home. It doesn't usually work. Wait at least a day. If you are interested in visiting the home, tell the seller that you are going to do some math and that in a few days you will send them an offer. Remember that in this case we are talking about wanting to get a significant discount on the price they are asking. If you agree with the starting price, obviously don't wait and close the transaction as soon as possible.

But okay, let's go back to the importance of waiting at least a day. You are creating an expectation (and a certain illusion obviously on the selling side). And for your part, you are lowering your emotions and therefore we already know that "when emotions go down, your rational thinking increases" or that "let the pillow do its job."

The next day or a few days later, you will present a lower offer to the selling party with the series of reasoning that we have already covered above. If you negotiate directly with the selling party, try to present the offer in person. Face to face. Face to face you will have more chances of having your offer accepted (yes, I know, you have to be braver and it takes more time. C'est la vie!

Why? Because it is harder for human beings to reject a proposal when face to face. Bring with you the reasons written on a sheet of paper. Lean on the sheet when you explain the offer. The sheet is very important. There is a reason (or several) why you are making that financial offer. And that argument is on paper.

I already know that it is much more efficient not to do it in person, and it also takes more courage. Investing time in a face to face I assure you that it increases your chances. If, on the other hand, you present the offer to the commercial agent, it is not so important that the meeting be in person (although it always helps) and, above all, ask the commercial agent to give a copy of your argument to set the price for the party. saleswoman. It is important.

This is within your control. Up to this point, everything depends on you. If you do it this way you will have increased the possibilities and you will be able to sleep peacefully at night because you have done your part well.

If the selling party declines the offer, be very polite and thank them for all the time invested or make a slight counterproposal. I say lightly because if you change the proposal radically you have lost all credibility in your argument and you are losing all options in the last phase that we will see below.

7.- The last bullet more than 100 days later.

The final phase is what occurs after 4-6 months. If at the end of those months the home is still for sale, contact the selling party and tell them that you want to resume your proposal: you are willing to raise it slightly if the selling party is willing to lower their initial claims.

In 100-180 days, the seller's expectations may have changed a lot. And if that happens, you will be there. If you have built trust and demonstrated seriousness and diligence, you will have options. Note that in any contact with the selling party you are "investing", you are leaving seeds that can germinate in the short or medium term future. Therefore, maintain impeccable conduct. Always.

When they tell you NO, don't see it as a defeat. Understand that NO as a part of the process. And like a seed you've planted. And that, in the future, if you have left many seeds, some will most likely be able to germinate.

One last important note about the method.

I like to be transparent and I can't stand those who sell smoke. The normal thing is that after doing this process and applying "the method", they do not accept your offer. Clear. What did you expect? You are trying to buy a home below the market price. And that is not easy.

Therefore, it is normal that it does not turn out well. But if you use the method I've taught you, you'll have a much better chance of being one of those "bargain" buyers who often sign for a home below market price in the best cities.

Remember, almost every day a home is sold at a good discount in the area or near where you want to buy. Embrace, grow, and learn from the process. Every day, there is a new game to play.

Take care of your head. Take care of those noes. Don't let them discourage you. Every NO you receive is a victory, because you have had the courage to submit a purchase offer and you will have learned something new. Look at it from this perspective.

Think long term and make a plan. Visit, analyze, do the numbers and offer. And again. That's the only secret.

CHAPTER 7 - THE IDEAL TENANT: METHODS FOR ENSURING SUCCESS

Tenant selection is probably one of the most important phases that exists for owners who rent our homes.

Aside from the headaches that an unsuitable tenant can cause, managing a bad tenant can lead to a substantial loss of profitability on the investment.

For these reasons, tenant selection is a process to which I dedicate the most time. I strictly follow the method I've designed, emphasizing the importance of having a structured approach. This methodology has evolved through my experiences with various tenants, including instances where mistakes were made.

I can already tell you that it is not an infallible method and it is also a method that can surely be improved. However, in my case, it works well because I believe the ratio of time invested to effectiveness is quite high.

Obviously investing more time could still improve, but overall, it probably won't pay off. Let's start with some basic principles that will put our heads in order before knowing the method in detail.

Basic principles when selecting your tenants.

- An empty apartment is better than a poorly occupied one. That is, you don't want to rush through this process. The same thing happens as with a job vacancy, it is better to have it empty than to fill it quickly with an incorrect profile.

- The method is effective whether you engage an agency to rent the home for you or if you handle the rental process directly. If you do it through an agency, you will have to get involved in the last steps.

- When you make a selection of people you can make mistakes. The only thing we intend with the method is to exponentially reduce your chances of error.

- The method works for both cheap homes and expensive homes with more limited demand. The only difference is that in homes with less demand you will need a somewhat longer process to create final competence (a critical step so that your emotional mind does not fool your rational mind with the belief that a candidate is good for the simple fact that they it's the only one).

- Like any method you will internalize it with practice.

- Since the responsibility is yours, feel free to adapt it to your circumstances (watch what you simplify).

- My "perfect tenant" is someone who has a long time horizon and who takes care of the home because he wants to live in it for many years. Maybe for you it is another profile. Maybe you are looking for someone who can pay you the most money possible in the short term and who won't hesitate to leave you six months' deposit? In my case I prefer to enter a little less, but have someone who feels the apartment is theirs. You can adapt the method to the priorities you are looking for in your "perfect tenant."

- And finally, remember that there is no more important phase in managing rental apartments than choosing a tenant. A poor choice in this regard will mean months or years of avoidable problems.

The 5-step method I use to find the "best possible tenant."

1-. Get quality VISITS on real estate portals: upload the ad on online portals with an approximate 3-5% discount compared to a competitive market price.

The first phase has a clear objective, which is to obtain potential interested parties in the apartment of the highest quality possible so that they can proceed to the next phase of interviews.

When uploading the ad, I clearly specify the hours in which they can call so that it does not interfere with my professional activity; some interested parties do not comply, by the way.

I upload the ad with a discount of 3-5% compared to the market value (the price must be adjusted to generate more demand), in the ad I put as much information as possible and specify the most relevant and critical information: the months of deposit and the fact that I am looking for tenants with financial solvency. In this step you should also clearly specify whether or not you as the owner allow pets.

A genuine candidate, truly interested in the apartment, will not hesitate to call according to the specified schedule. Obviously, I try to put wide strips and I always raise the floor on a Saturday since the first two days are when the calls are concentrated. In this way, that first weekend I already begin to filter through the next phase that I explain below.

2-. Get the first calls that meet the requirements that we detail in the advertisement and start filtering them.

The first phone call is very important since it is possible to extract a lot of information. The first thing I do is listen to the questions that the potential tenant asks to understand what they have not understood well about the advertisement.

Normally many people ask things that they have already seen simply so that you can give them a little more information about it. In any case, if the first question that a potential tenant asks you is about whether it is possible to reduce the two or three months that I ask for deposit or guarantee, or if it is possible to reduce the rent of the apartment, you can already begin to suspect certain priorities or difficulties of the potential tenant. When the tenant has finished presenting his questions, two things can happen:

- The first is that you have already ruled it out based on the questions you have asked. Especially if many of the questions have been related to the deposit or the price. In that case, I thank him or her and tell him that the visits will begin next weekend (if that is the case) and that if I am interested in him or her making a visit, I would answer the same phone number that is calling me.
- In. In the event that the conversation has been normal and it seems that there is genuine interest and that it has not been self-dismissed, I start with my battery of open questions (open questions always give us a wide horizon of knowledge about the other person).

List of questions to ask in the first phone call

- Why do you want to live in this apartment?
- Why in this area of the city?
- Where have you lived before and for what reasons do you want to change?
- What percentage of your income are you going to dedicate to rent?

The final question during the phone interview, provided the candidate hasn't disqualified themselves earlier, is always:

- How long do you think you are going to live in this apartment?

When asking this last question, obviously do not indicate in advance that you are interested in long-term tenants. The question should be open and as if it had no major importance. If the potential tenant is relaxed (try to create a friendly and close "telephone climate") they will tend to answer you honestly.

This last question, along with your personal situation, tells us a lot about the chances of you being a long-term tenant or just passing through.

In our case we are looking for very long-term rentals. In fact, we prefer them even if it means we have to lower the rental price of the home a little.

We love to think that in some of the apartments the tenant thinks that they cannot leave their home because it would be difficult for them to find an apartment with that good quality-price ratio. That (along with the creation of greater demand) is the reason for slightly lowering the rental price by a few percentage points.

I know some of you may be thinking I'm giving away some money. Could be. At present, I highly value my time on an hourly basis, and I prefer to invest it in activities I am passionate about, such as spending time with my family, traveling, or dedicating it to my primary profession. And I know that if I can choose a tenant my management time drops radically. What do you prefer? Should you be the one who chooses the tenant or should the tenant choose you because you have no other alternatives?

You must play with the probabilities to increase/decrease those of those variables that you want to maximize/minimize: length of stay, risk of non-payment, housing care, incident management, rental price...

If you have passed all the filters in the form of questions (in that case I have invested about ten minutes), we make an appointment to visit the home (or if it is not yet available - which usually happens because I rent the home for two or three weeks before the other tenant has left - we agree to close the week before the home is available to visit). I saved his information and a day before sent him a message to remind him of the scheduled visit. Sometimes it's incredible how people don't keep appointments and don't even let them know.

3-. The first visit to the apartment of potentially interesting tenants.

If the advertisement is well done (good photos and a lot of descriptive information) and is exhaustive in the information it contains, normally in half - or more - of the occasions) after the first visit the potential tenant will want to rent the home. The same "clean" or "dirty" kitchen gives a completely different appearance to the home. Don't forget to take care of this part.

It is at that moment when we are going to ask you some important questions on a professional level to get to know you much better. We must especially know the amount and security of your income, the type of company you work for and the date of seniority. We are not going to ask for any payroll yet. But on the economic issue many will fall for obvious reasons.

When I clearly see that the income is not sufficient, I explain it to them, arguing that there are other candidates who have greater security in paying the rent. In the event that the information you provide us fits and the rental amount does not exceed 30-35% of the tenants' total income, we could move on to the next phase.

We will tell you that there are already several interested parties in the apartment (as long as it is true, obviously), we will ask for your full name and surname and we will also announce that in the next few days (usually the following weekend) there will be the final selection of the tenant and We have already assigned you a day and time so that you can plan and have a date in your head.

In the meantime, I will look for information on the potential tenant. Especially on LinkedIn and Twitter, which is where most professional information is usually found. Obviously, there are profiles in which no information is found, but in others there is very valuable information.

It is very important not to discriminate against potential tenants for any reason. But remember that as an owner, the more information you have, the better decision you can make.

4 and 5-. Second visit and final selection. Final interview in the home you are going to rent.

In the process of second visits to the home, I like to at least get five visits that are very interested and really want to move forward with the rental. This second visit is a visit that many of you will think is not necessary, but for me it is the most important.

The first thing is that by calling them at a time when sooner or later there are more very interested visitors, we will put the tenant in a mental state of wanting something that is in high demand. After informing them that there are several finalists, I announce the following: «Today I only see candidates. "I will make the final decision in the next five days."

When I utter that phrase, I achieve several objectives. Firstly, I'm setting the expectation upfront that a decision won't be made today. So, I reduce tension.

And the second and most important thing is that I gain five days to negotiate the contract with my preferred candidate and if he falls out for any reason, I can continue with my second preferred candidate without him being considered "the second course."

Furthermore, five days normally gives me time to sign the contract (or leave it more than just a word), so when I answer the interested interviewees, I can inform them that in the end the apartment has been awarded to another tenant and give them certain reasons. basics of the reason for my choice.

Establishing a scenario where the candidate understands they are not the sole contender and that there are several others is crucial for the final negotiation. This way when you finalize the details of the contract you can always negotiate "reasonable things" with much more force.

In this appointment, if the house is furnished, we sit on the sofa (if it is not, we have the conversation standing) and basically after a brief introduction I announce that I have a problem and that I need your help.

My problem is the following:

There are five potential tenants who want the home and I like them all: Could you help me decide? Why should I choose you (or you)? It is a very difficult question. Very open. Many tenants are left standing at the beginning. But I assure you that you see many things in the candidates' answers.

During this final phase, my main objective is to understand the 'values' or behavioral traits of the person who will be living in one of our homes. After you've shared your reasons for why I should consider renting to you, my next step is to explore your past experiences with challenging situations.

I allow them to share examples of problems or points of contention with the previous owner and explain how they resolved them. I'm aware it resembles a job interview, but similar to recruiting, we understand that selecting individuals can be challenging. And therefore, having a clear methodology and a clear script of questions helps us obtain better results and select much better.

Finally, we talk about future problems. I tell him things that will (probably) happen and ask him who will have to take care of those problems.

The first question is always the following: Is it necessary   carry out air conditioning maintenance? The tenant's answer is yes, usually. The next question is: How often does it have to be done? Here the festival of different answers can begin.

And the last question is: Who should pay the air conditioning maintenance? Here, many do not know the law. It is obviously the tenant (maintenance is always the tenant; repairs are always the owner unless there is misuse by the tenant). Just because they get the answer wrong doesn't mean they won't rent the home. Not at all. I just want to understand how he reacts to questions that are uncomfortable and not easy to answer.

By the way, I always write about the air conditioning by contract. This way there are no doubts or surprises. As well as the waste expenses that the tenant must take care of. All those "little problems" that you can anticipate and that have a very clear answer, better write them "verbatim" in the contract. You will save yourself unnecessary discussions. It is the best for the relationship.

What if they are young tenants who are new and have no experience renting? There the values are even more decisive. It is normal that if they rent for the first time, they do not know much about how the tenant-landlord relationship works. In those cases, I even focus the conversation more towards the future. I also "invent" future problems to understand how they can react in different situations.

One of the final questions (if they are not inexperienced tenants) is always this: Could you provide me with the telephone number of the last owners of your previous rental homes so that I can request references? The answers I've received to this question have been so much fun!

Additional considerations regarding final interviews.

In the final visits/interviews I am always with someone so I can share opinions. I always ask the family member or friend who accompanies me during the interview session for their opinion after interviewing each potential candidate. We exchange our opinions if we have time between visits.

At the end of all interviews is when it helps me the most to be accompanied. I ask my family member/friend to give me her list of preferred candidates before I give her my list. And I always ask him the main reasons for his selection. And this whole process continues to give me much more information.

Ultimately, I am prepared to make the most informed decision possible, given the factors within my control up to this point. If I have done this work, I am calm because what depended on me, I have already done. The input is already there. Now we need to ensure that the output is with us and that the tenant we select is really "a good tenant".

We have done our job, which is what is really important.

If you rent long term and expand your properties, time will prove the "method" right. You will see that by following the method the life of an owner is much better. Much calmer and with many fewer incidents that could keep you awake.

This is one of those investments in time that has a great return. Investing a little more time at the beginning can mean three, five, seven, ten... years of "peace of mind." Some additional aspects that help me rule out potential tenants:

- If he starts with lies, even small ones, I rule out the candidate without thinking.
- If you want to negotiate very hard on any very relevant aspect, I usually rule it out, especially if your way of negotiating is very aggressive.
- If there is no consistency in your previous history or you explain to me that you had major problems with the previous owners, I also rule it out (it seems like a lie, but there are potential tenants who explain to you that the previous owners were despotic).

Final notes/details about the method:

1. When renting apartments in the low price range (normally below 700 or 800 dollars) there is a lot of demand. You have already observed that the key to the method is to generate a lot of interest in the market to have a lot of demand.

2. It is up to you whether you want to look at defaulter lists (ASNEF lists), or not, depending on the type of tenant you rent to.

3. When asking for references from previous tenants, if the tenant

has lived in several homes, try to ask for all references. In my case I don't usually call. The filter is usually the answer to your request (if there are many excuses, bad sign).

4. Sometimes, it may happen, that you have a perfect candidate who is on the low income limit. On occasion, I have been transparent with the candidate and told him that he would need to increase the rent by 5% to be able to pay the non-payment insurance. In this way, a great candidate "for values" can win the game against a much better candidate economically, but with, a priori, "worse values."

5. The photos and description of the home must be impeccable (you can invest in professional photos for a relatively low price - less than $250).

6. Use more than one online real estate portal and you will still have extra demand.

7. Paying an extra demand (you can position your ad better by paying) on real estate portals if your apartment is not at a correct market price is counterproductive (you burn it). If the price is right, it can help you get even more potential tenants, obviously.

8. If you rent it directly without an agency, there is one less commission to pay by the tenant. This can also help you create a little more demand. Highlight it in the ad.

9. Don't be like many companies when interviewing candidates. Always inform all candidates that you are not moving forward with the process. Be polite and transparent (you will help the candidate).

10. On the day of signing, obviously I do not hand over keys until I have proof of the transfer made with the months of deposit and the first month (normally we do it "live", with the mobile).

11. If you plan well, you can rent an apartment in less than one or two weeks, even if the previous tenant has left the apartment without prior notice.

"The perfect tenant"?

At the end of the day, it is important to understand that the method is obviously not infallible. If the tenant goes wrong, having done a good job beforehand, we can at least tell ourselves that we have done our part. We are going to focus, as always, on doing what depends on us as best as possible.

And then? The new life as a landlord when you have a good tenant.

Sometimes I get a message from one of the tenants. I see the notification on the screen and I'm extremely lazy to open it. When a tenant sends you a WhatsApp (almost) it is never to congratulate you on your birthday. In general, it is to inform you of any of the following incidents:

- The neighbor upstairs makes a lot of noise. Can you tell him something?
- The heater has broken (can you believe that on the same day two heaters in two of our different homes broke.
- My mother is not well and I want to leave the apartment before the minimum period has expired.
- I want to put a longer hose on the shower so I can shower sitting down.

All of the above are real cases.

At these points there are two issues in my opinion to comment on: The first is that in 95% of the problems, I will never visit the apartment; I avoid it. My time is worth much more. And that's why when I select tenants, I think about how they are going to solve the problems themselves. Obviously when it's my turn to pay, I pay. And I have the phone numbers of reference specialists that I can send quickly.

Even the older couple convinced me that their daughter was there to help them. And when there is a problem I talk to her daughter, she is lovely and between the two parties we solve everything quickly.

The second crucial aspect is that I consistently strive to see things from the tenant's perspective. That's why I try to solve the problem (through others) as quickly as possible.

Keep in mind that owning and renting an apartment today is more manageable compared to the challenges faced in the nineties. Do you know why? Because of the technological tools we now have: WhatsApp, Marketplace for online professionals, mobile banking, online portals.

Don't forget, at the end of the day you can already sense that the only way to find the "perfect tenant" is to never stop in the search to become a "perfect owner." If you don't give, why should the other party? Strive to be a better owner each day, and over time, you'll attract better tenants.

At this point in the book, you can already guess that I am passionate about real estate investment in rental homes, as well as other types of investments that we have already talked about in my other book. And I am passionate about it because there is a large part of the final result, the profitability obtained, that depends on the management we do as investors.

FINAL REFLECTION

You don't have to believe literally all the strategies and methodologies that I have told you. At the end of the day, that's what has worked for me. Make necessary adaptations, as these strategies and methods are not perfect, and different approaches may have worked in the past, producing good results.

In any case, the long-term vision is almost indisputable in my investment strategy, whether as real estate investment or investment in fixed and variable income through investment funds and ETFs as we saw in "Financial freedom". We have to understand that nothing is built in a day, but the effect of compound interest, both in the stock market and in real estate investments, is unstoppable.

Rushing and letting emotions guide you typically do not lead to long-term success. There are different ways to make money when investing in real estate. Buying homes to rent is without a doubt my favorite. Although it is not the only one. Buying cheap, renovating well and then selling can also work. Although it is another type of investment.

And you already know that you can't be 'good' at everything. Winning gold in the 100 meters and simultaneously in the mile is impossible.

Keep in mind that you are not in competition with anyone; your only competition is with yourself. Don't be too hard on yourself. You are unique and irreplaceable. Embrace your uniqueness and remember to enjoy your time.

Knowledge in real estate investment and action must go hand in hand. **Start today and learn as you journey towards financial freedom through long-term rental property investing.**

If you enjoyed the book, I also recommend 'Financial Freedom: Investing guide to getting rich step by step with index funds, ETFs, and real estate' to complement your passive income. These forms of investing are what have allowed my family and me to achieve financial freedom and can be the way to achieve your own.

If you enjoyed the book, kindly share your experience by leaving a comment on Amazon. Your opinion is crucial! If you liked it and, above all, if you found it useful, you will contribute to giving it more visibility so that more people can benefit from these ideas. I also encourage you to write a comment if you didn't like it, so others won't waste their time and I will improve the book for future editions.

Thank you for being part of this project!

Until next time!

Rental property investing. Part of Passive Income Guides. Alexander S.

Date of 1st edition: December 2023

www.ingramcontent.com/pod-product-compliance
Lightning Source LLC
Chambersburg PA
CBHW032028290526
45786CB00011B/1034